LOOKING WITHIN:

WHY WE DON'T SAY NO
BUT SHOULD

LOOKING WITHIN:

WHY WE DON'T SAY NO BUT SHOULD

LEKEVIE JOHNSON

Seraph Books

Inspired: Lekevie Johnson

Copyright © 2020 by Lekevie Johnson

ISBN Paperback: 978-1-941711-25-5
ISBN E-Book: 978-1-941711-26-2
Library of Congress Control Number: 2020920677

10 9 8 7 6 5 4 3 2 1

Copyediting by Alyssa M. Curry
Cover design by Alyssa M. Curry
Cover photo by Aaron Lamont Curry

CONTENTS

INTRODUCTION

Have you taken the time to evaluate yourself before judging others? Are you exempt from having made poor decisions, or displaying negative behaviors or emotions because something wasn't aligned with what you believe, wanted, or felt you deserved? Our decisions, behaviors, and emotional health tell us a great deal about who we are spiritually and as individuals.

During this time, where racism is being encouraged and the Coronavirus is causing widespread fear, illness, and death, we must pause and assess our behaviors and contributions to our current climate. We must draw on the strongest attributes of our upbringing and recognize who we have become. For many reasons, we have an obligation to ourselves and to one another, to look within and determine how we can improve mentally, physically, emotionally, and spiritually. We have that same obligation to others, such as our children, loved ones, friends, and colleagues.

We have the tendency to learn more about ourselves when we are isolated from others. Often, we are too busy with our normal routines to pay attention to ourselves and what's going on around us. Now, we are forced to look out our windows, watch the news, and feel the plight of our brothers, sisters, friends, colleagues, and strangers. This certainly has become more relevant today as we face the deadly and destructive plight of racism and Coronavirus. Our ability to adjust and adapt is based upon who we are. When we look within, we can discover the truth about our faith or the vulnerability that we possess. In Looking Within, this is evident when the serpent engages Eve. Solid faith eliminates vulnerability.

The fundamental difference between what is right and wrong is critical to changing and improving oneself. When I think about growing up in the Mississippi Delta, I remember questioning our environment. If you want an example of separation, look at neighborhoods and churches. The reality is that individuals have made separation okay.

The important piece of self-improvement is accountability. Accountability works best before your actions and choices are put into motion. If you don't acknowledge your behavior beforehand, the conclusion can be damaging. Make the decision to look within and determine where your morals and values lie and what impact you want to have on the lives of others as well as your own.

ACKNOWLEDGEMENTS

First and foremost, I am grateful to God who gave me the vision, endurance, and patience to complete this project. I am also appreciative of my village who was instrumental in my growth and helped me to become the man I am today. Special thanks and appreciation to my wife, Rochelle, and my children Kaleb and Kennedy. Completing this book is not possible without your support, sacrifice, and push. This book is dedicated to each of you. To my mom, thank you for your prayers, your constant and unwavering support. Thank you for giving me life. To my hard-working, strong, and spiritual grandmother, I honor your memory and your legacy. To M.S., thank you for grooming and investing in me to make this project successful from start to finish. Last but not least to my church family, The Hill, thank you for allowing me to serve as your leader and your continuous love.

1.

SELF-EXAMINATION

"The steps of a good man are ordered by the Lord and he delighted in his way."

Psalms 37:23 (KJV)

~

In the Bible, Genesis is the beginning of everything. There is a great deal to learn when dissecting what occurred. When we take under consideration everything that God granted Adam and Eve, it is important to ask why they would have desired anything more. The answer to that question is spiritual and addresses how God created humanity. When God created humankind, He did so by giving Adam and Eve the ability to be appreciative, productive, and make decisions. The discovery of why Eve and Adam failed spiritually in the garden is from these core truths. I've named Eve first because the issue began with her, and life in the garden headed for chaos because of her decision to entertain the serpent. When chaos arrives, it's because people are distracted. The failure of Adam and Eve was allowing the serpent to distract them, which kept them from productivity. It was God who gave Adam and Eve an assignment about production. He told them to be fruitful and multiply and to name His creation. God knew they had the ability to produce, which is why He instructed them to stay away from anything unproductive. This leads humanity to the place of free will.

Life and productivity are about spirituality and whether humanity is willing to follow the plan that God has for their lives. In the sight of God, Adam and Eve are both good. The issue they faced was not executing the plan God had clearly given them. Submitting oneself spiritually to God for consistent guidance is a problem that humanity faces; yet, it is not about seeking God's direction about things that are in His permissive will. For example, God doesn't care if you become a doctor or artist. He grants humanity the ability to make that decision. Though, He does care if you take the serpent's advice over His. The similarity between these examples is the ability to choose. Every choice that humanity makes should begin with the question, Is my choice in alignment with the Word of God? When your spiritual antenna remains up, then a clear remembrance of God's plan is natural for your life. Staying in the presence of God and continuing in the journey of studying His Word is how you keep your spiritual antenna up.

When Eve decided to listen to the serpent, she entertained desires that appealed to the natural man and not the spiritual man. The serpent told Eve to eat from the forbidden place, but there is no record that the serpent had done so. Eve took advice from the serpent who was merely keeping her from being productive. The consistent inner battle that humanity faces is whether they should satisfy the natural man or strengthen the spiritual man. The reality is you can't do both. Humanity can't listen to the serpent (natural) and follow God's plan (spiritual) because they are contradictory to one another. More often than not, the natural man will focus on self-gratification and not a true self-examination. Before Eve ate from that forbidden place for self-gratification, she should have determined why she had that desire to do so. Before Adam accepted Eve's invitation to eat from the forbidden place, he should have questioned the reason he desired to do so.

The Apostle Paul gives a strong principle to utilize in self-examination. "Casting down imaginations, and every high thing that exalteth itself against the knowledge of God and bringing into captivity every thought to the obedience of Christ" (2 Corinthians 10:5 KJV). This nugget of wisdom could have led Eve to tell the serpent no. This same principle could have led Adam to tell Eve no. Two opportunities to complete a self-examination before making their decision were ignored. Not only did Adam and Eve ignore the opportunities to complete self-examinations, so did we.

I was raised in a little town in Mississippi called Symonds. Though a small, poverty-stricken community, it was generous with its bean, rice, and cotton fields in the dog days of summer. Regardless of how hard I searched, I couldn't find Symonds on a map when I was a kid. Other than family and friends, there was barely anything there. I'd walk out the front door, down the four small porch steps of our two-bedroom house, take thirty steps into the slightest breeze wafting cotton parachutes, and end up on my maternal grandmother Ruthie's doorstep. Not much farther across the narrow, dusty rock road was my great-aunt Hattie Bell's small brick house. Hattie Bell was my grandmother's older sister and her presence was so soft, I'd light up as soon as my hazel eyes met her. My cousins lived with their mom next door to Hattie Bell's house. My fourth cousin Mark lived with Hattie Bell right next to them. Living that close to family was practically the same as living under one roof. We were a tight-knit group, all close in age, which kept us doing chores, going to school, and playing together. Out in that isolated, unincorporated community is where each of us learned to drive—before the legal age. My oldest cousin often drove us three miles to the nearest corner store for candy and snacks, but the drive alone was the fun part.

Although quiet and curious by nature, I stayed in the mix of things. I had a lot of questions as a kid, but I wasn't perceived as talkative because I kept them to myself. One of them was, why would anyone want to live in that secluded area? And who would want to wake up in the middle of the night to chop wood and tend to the fire in the coldest of winter? I would come to learn that we didn't have the best house, cars, or clothing. It didn't bother me because I didn't think anyone had much in Symonds anyway. Although it was a frustrating life at the time, my roots taught me something that our current society has failed to embrace.

The importance of seeing the value in others has led to a huge disconnect among humanity.

I affectionately called my grandmother Ruthie "Grannie," and she was everything to me. Grannie had a medium frame, broad shoulders, stood 5'9" and was strong. Her silver, shoulder-length hair was almost always covered with a scarf. One with a green, white, and yellow pattern was her favorite. I could always spot her in the distance just by that scarf. When I got closer, it seemed like the sun made her smooth, medium-brown complexion and black eyes glisten beautifully, but it was her soul shining through. Grannie didn't laugh much, but I knew when she was happy and unhappy. She was spiritual, hard-working, and a disciplinarian to her core. Grannie invested in her grandchildren by teaching us what she wanted us to know. I could never use the excuse that I didn't know how to do something because she had already shown me how to do it. When we started cutting grass, it was Grannie who bought the gas, poured it in the lawnmower, started it, and showed us how she wanted it cut by cutting it while we watched. The first time I cut grass, she told me, "Put on long sleeves."

I looked at my cousin and mumbled, "Why do I have to wear long sleeves? It's hot."

She overheard and replied, "That's why! It's hot. Protect your skin."

Grannie had a powerful presence, which didn't come from a formal education beyond her primary years; it came from life. Every time I saw Grannie, she was working or doing something constructive. This lesson of building toward a goal was her approach to life. Perhaps a lesson from Grannie is needed in our communities today where destruction has become too normal at times. She was so busy building that she didn't have time for destructive energy. There was no reason to ask her why she stayed busy because she let it be known that "Lazy people starve." I can't recall ever seeing her out of control anytime something frustrating happened. She said, "People who scream and yell are not in charge." If Grannie told me to cut the grass by the time she got home and I didn't, I knew I was in trouble. One time, she pulled up in her car, went straight to the shed to get the lawnmower, and cut the grass herself wearing Wrangler jeans and a buttoned-up plaid shirt.

"Grannie, I've got it," I tried to explain.

"No, you don't," she said, ignoring my plea. "You'll get it later, though."

She'd wash the clothes, put them in baskets, and tell us to hang them out on the line. If she started hanging them herself because we did our own thing, it was over. Grannie's voice was as calm as a cotton field without a trace of wind when she'd say, "You haven't done anything I've asked you to do. Go out to the bush and get a switch. If it's a little one, you're going to regret it. If I have to go outside and pick it myself—that's going to be a problem for you."

She helped raise us to be respectful and disciplined so we didn't talk back. If we earned that punishment, we obediently got that switch and took it. Anything less than being respectful and disciplined was unacceptable. When I did what I was asked to do, Grannie was in a good space with me. I could tell by the way she'd gently squeeze my nose. That was her way of saying I love you.

Grannie worked at the Alabama Metal Products Company where they manufactured sheet metal, furniture parts, and cabinets. My mother, Joyce, worked long hours as a food service manager at the State Park. And my father, Lloyde, was a pastor. Mom said that Dad had a solid income from the church, but we lived like he was trying to make ends meet—and those ends never met because we didn't see any of his earnings. He'd bring home bologna or ham and a loaf of Wonder Bread but when that was gone, it was gone. It was Mom and Grannie who made sure we had what we needed.

Nearly 30 yards from our house, Dad constructed a building made out of tin. It didn't look like much, but he used it as a body shop to fix engines and restore old cars whenever he came home. Dad smoked like a chimney and when his burnt orange 1971 Cadillac Deville was parked by the shop, the lingering stench of his Kool 100s let me know I'd find his 6'2" frame either beneath a car or hovering under its hood. If Dad wasn't working on a car, he dressed sharp and wore dress slacks and a white button-up shirt everywhere he went. His hair was typically neatly parted and combed to the side and his dark complexion was illuminated by his striking smile. It didn't take long before his reputation as a mechanic grew and his makeshift shop turned into a junkyard. Stacks of tires, rusty parts, and all types of cars either waiting for repairs, broken down, or in pieces surrounded the place, and one of them was usually ours.

Mr. Bill was one of the wealthiest men in the Mississippi Delta and my grandfather, Virgie, was a heavy equipment operator on his farmland. Mr. Bill bought the land and then used it as payment for his workers. After more than twenty years of service, Mr. Bill deeded almost five acres to my grandfather. Although Grandfather left us, our homes on that land were bought and paid for by hard work. From what I'd seen and the stories I'd been told, my family possessed a strong work ethic. I was barely ten when my brother Frentrous and I started working for Mr. Bill. He paid each of us twenty-five dollars a week to use a hoe and chop the tall weeds that grew around the cotton, so it took less time for the laborers to harvest. We worked Monday through Friday from 5 a.m. until 8 a.m. during the summer. On Fridays, Mr. Bill would go to the bank to get fifty dollars in quarters and nickels, divide them into two plastic sandwich bags, and pay us. I'd shake my head and take my earnings wondering why Mr. Bill didn't think we would have preferred dollars. This was our early introduction to racism in the south; even when we had completed the work, degrading us with a bag of change was the reminder of who was big and who was small. In our current climate of police brutality and systematic racism, we are still experiencing the same discord. This must change.

Symonds was a place without secrets. It was so small, there was no place to hide one. It seemed as though everyone made it a mission to keep up on everything that happened.

If my brother or I did something mischievous in school, it wasn't out of the ordinary to get off the bus and have one of the neighbors standing there with their eyes narrowed and arms folded across their chest, waiting to hold us accountable for our behavior. I couldn't help but wonder where people were getting their information from because—they were right. I was a self-proclaimed professional rock thrower. If I so much as picked up a rock to throw at something, somebody knew about it almost as fast as I threw it. I wasn't trying to do any harm; I was just having fun hitting things—like houses—because there wasn't much else to do. The only thing I had to look forward to in Symonds was driving fifteen miles to town to go to Walmart, Fred's Dollar Store, McDonald's or McKay's. Given we didn't have a wide selection of food, clothing, furniture, cars, or anything else, that meant we had the same things that everyone around us had. At eleven years old, my logic was that if we bought our washing machine from McKay's, and he didn't have a factory behind his store, someone was supplying him. I didn't have any proof, but my father was relentless in preaching about faith and that was my motivation for believing there was more to life than what I could see.

In Mississippi and the South, people went to church one Sunday each month. Some pastors had multiple congregations, and my father had four in his monthly rotation. Pleasant Grove was his closest church, just two and a half miles from Symonds. The other Sundays we traveled to Duncan, Shelby, and then Parchman, which had the largest prison farm in Mississippi. Driving to those cities is where I saw paved roads, two-story homes, and nicer neighborhoods. Seeing those places created a broader curiosity as to what else I was missing. Since there were other communities built outside of the dusty rock road we lived on, I wanted to know why our community was limited to the single-story brick homes that we lived in. I couldn't ask my parents or Grannie because asking "why" was the ultimate sin when I was growing up. I thought it would feed my curiosity; they perceived it as being disrespectful to elders. But that didn't shut down my inquisitiveness. I was internally driven to find out what the other options were because I wanted to have access to them.

Sunday mornings were something. If we rode with Dad, a twenty to thirty-minute argument between my parents was guaranteed. When we rode with Mom, it was peaceful. Once we arrived at church, everything was vocal. Dad had the church folks screaming, crying, hollering—having a high-spirited Baptist fit. The choirs were especially good because my father had an ear for music, which he used to assemble the choir in each church. Back then, his churches were considered to be a nice size. His church was swelling, and the smoldering heat rose to the rafters. When Dad disrupted the service by singing "A Cabin in Glory," I'd sit there singing right along with him, "I want you to build me a cabin in glory where I can rest my weary soul." Dad wasn't solely an animated entertainer. He was a phenomenal singer, and that drew people to him. With those two skills, he fervently held everyone's attention in church. Once he started singing or preaching, people moved like nothing I'd ever seen before.

My father was gifted and he relied on that particular set of skills to keep that job. But the man I saw in church every Sunday wasn't my father. He was nothing like him. Dad treated the people in his congregations better than his family. Although my father was a pastor, what he practiced and preached were two different things. When the conversation got heated between him and Mom, I wasn't able to say or do anything about it because we were raised not to interfere in grown folks' business. Dad was preaching to people about how they should behave and live, but he didn't appear to study his own behaviors and motivations for them.

As I grew older, I found that my father said yes to things he clearly should have said no to—given he innately knew right from wrong. It was my father's inability to appreciate what he already had that caused him to desire more of what was not intended for him. My father was our modern-day Eve because his appetite created chaos and impacted everyone connected to him. I was halfway through elementary school when I thought I was called to be a preacher like my father. However, time and reflection brought discernment. I stopped listening to that calling.

One Sunday at my father's church in Duncan I sat in the first pew waiting for service to commence when I witnessed Mom's attention shift to a particular woman who sang in the women's quartet with her. The woman was slowly strutting down the aisle in a big black hat and a yellow dress like she was the first lady of the church. She gave my mother an evil grin and brushed past Mom, seating herself in the choir without saying a word. I could tell by the abrupt change in my mother's peaceful demeanor that the woman's presence was upsetting. Moments later, Mom got up and walked over to my father, discreetly attempting to confront him about bringing that woman, his mistress, to church while his children were there. Dad said a few words and without any fear of consequences, he drew his hand back and slapped Mom right in front of the entire congregation. No one other than the Deacon said anything. The Deacon walked over to my mother and suggested, "Mrs. Johnson, why don't you and the boys go home?" The culture and the environment were supportive of the pastor regardless of anything else. Dad was good with the powers that be, the politics, and finagling while we suffered through the embarrassment of it all. There wasn't a high level of integrity, and I didn't think they cared about Dad any more than they did Mom. He was an entertainer, and they cared about his talent keeping the church going strong.

Despite the calling I felt on my young life, every time I watched my father, I thought, if this is what Christianity is about and who God is—then who wants Him. According to scripture, my father was never qualified to be a pastor. "For if a man know not how to rule his own house, how shall he take care of the church of God?" Timothy: 1:3-5. Watching my father gave me a personal template of what not to do; therefore, I disconnected from God.

After that incident, my father didn't come home much, but when he was home, things were tense between my parents. I'd become accustomed to the way things were because I never expected anything to change. It was our life. Sometimes, our pasts affect the way we treat others and the paths we choose to take.

In August of 1985, Frentrous and I got off the school bus for our normal transfer to Mom's Grand Prix. Mom was waiting for us with both hands gripping the steering wheel while the car idled like she was in a hurry. Her short, brown hair was curly and looked pretty against her caramel complexion, but Mom seemed different. Regardless of what was going on she was often smiling, and I never understood how that was possible. This time, I didn't see her gold tooth center mass because she wasn't smiling. I opened the car door and climbed in only to slide my butt against the suitcases piled up on the backseat. Without any explanation, Mom glanced in her rearview mirror and told us, "We're going." I solemnly nodded my head. When I closed the car door, my eyes involuntarily fell shut. I couldn't look as Mom hit the gas and pulled away from our life.

Mom wasn't a woman of many words, but those words she said were meaningful. When she spoke, it was always something we should listen to. One of the things I love most about Mom is that she was always very affectionate. I got that from her, which is why it was so hard leaving Grannie. So hard. I'd seen and heard enough from my parents to know if she had to pack up and leave without Frentrous and me saying goodbye to anyone, Mom was running for her life. I didn't know if Mom had spoken to Grannie, and they agreed it was the best decision, but my mother didn't ask my brother and me how we felt. I couldn't understand why we were suddenly uprooted from our family, friends, and the only home we'd ever known. I'd grown used to their routine. Mom had stayed after everything my father had done; it became my normal. There had to be another option. Why didn't my father leave instead? He was gone most of the time anyway. His routine was to come by more than he came home. He'd drop off some bologna, sliced ham, and a couple loaves of bread so we had food. It didn't last long, which is the reason we ate at Grannie's. What people saw wasn't who my father was at home or to God. Couldn't he see what he was doing to his family? Did he care? I didn't know what my mother's plans were or how she would take care of us on her own, but I didn't need to worry about that because Mom was like her mother—a woman of amazing strength and a prayer warrior. She had to be trusting God. That's all it could be.

Seven hours later, I opened my eyes to find Mom driving through the smooth streets of St. Louis with the sweltering heat of August taking its toll on our car. She turned onto St. Louis Avenue with smoke billowing from beneath the light grey hood while the car left its trail of coolant. Certain we'd make it to our destination, Mom leaned her head away from the smoke threatening her view and kept driving while Frentrous and I took in the sights with our mouths agape. Big, beautiful, brick homes lined both sides of the street.

and none of them were the same. Some houses had two front doors, others had balconies overlooking the street. The color of their brick exteriors ranged from shades of brown to deep burgundy. The sidewalk ran all the way down the street into the subtle transition of a grocery store, clothing stores, various retail shops, and other businesses. Gas stations, stoplights, stop signs, cars, and buses were everywhere. People were more fashionable than I'd ever seen. I'd been in communities my father pastored, but they were nothing like what I was seeing now. I adjusted my black eyeglass frames and took in all the amazing options that would be sure to tempt anyone.

The car made it to Mom's older sister's two-story red brick duplex on St. Louis Ave, but it wasn't going any further. Aunt Doris was kind enough to let us move in with her, Uncle Dannie, and their three children Anthony, Angel, and Lil' Dannie. The three of us shared the basement of their home toting nothing but the clothing we left with.

After just a few weeks, I could tell that being at Aunt Doris's was healthier for Mom. She wasn't tense or upset. Mom was quiet as though she was still trying to figure things out. I'd often find her perched on the edge of the twin bed with her KJV white and gold Bible in her hands. Regardless of what was going on, Mom stayed connected to God. I wasn't the only one impacted by the change. After having left her husband and everything she knew and loved behind, Mom seemed to appreciate being there with Aunt Doris. It was obvious to me that my mother valued having another opportunity to set her life on a healthier path—void of abuse and public humiliation. I knew my mother missed Grannie and her family the same as me, and her adjustment to the changes coincided with her decision.

Although my mother accepted the consequences, it didn't work that way for me. I felt displaced and disconnected from my life as if something had been taken from us. I didn't have what I needed. I couldn't go to Grannie's or talk to my uncles, Michael and Ronald. That laughter had ended, and I didn't have them to help sharpen my athletic skills. They were a healthy part of my life, and that support was gone. My game console, toys, TV, guitar, keyboard, drums, and the rest of my personal belongings were left behind, too. I no longer shared a bedroom with Frentrous or had a space of my own. My environment and routine had changed significantly. We didn't sit down for meals or discuss what happened throughout our day, which meant we were no longer monitored or held responsible for our actions the same as before. I looked at the way I dressed compared to the other kids at school and realized I didn't have much at all. I wore jeans with holes at the knees, and they weren't distressed on purpose. My shirts were faded and my white gym shoes were old. My overall appearance garnered a lot of negative attention. Back home, I made do with what I had to work with and I fit in just fine. In St. Louis, I had to find a way to fit and adjust to life, so I created my new routine and made it fun by dealing myself a hand of more freedom and less accountability.

Mom was organized and focused on handling her responsibilities in St. Louis. I never heard her complain about anything, not even when the car broke down. She got us settled in our new school and found a job at the convenience store catty-corner from Aunt Doris's house. The next thing I knew, we had a church home, but I felt like I was going through the motions.

Since Frentrous and I were four years apart, he was in high school while I was in the seventh grade. I was taller, but his frame was wider, and our personalities seemed to hedge on being opposite, which made me miss my family even more. I didn't know anyone in school, and that contributed to making my first few weeks pretty rough. I was angry for being uprooted, and, as a result of my anger, I got into fights. They were those good fights, where the news spread throughout the student body and everyone came to see if the bully would add another victim to his list or get what he had coming. I wasn't the bully. I was the target. My clothing was one thing, but what made things worse for me was that I had problems seeing out of my left eye because it never developed properly. When I had surgery on that eye, as odd as it seemed, I was happy because, at that time, uncle Ronald and Michael brought Grannie to St. Louis. Even with my eye patched up, I was back to normal for those three days. The doctor told my mother that it would be a process of multiple surgeries before I'd literally see any improvement. My mother could only manage the one surgery and, as a result, my eye wandered and crossed. I had to wear a pair of thick, cheap eyeglasses that the state supplied. We didn't have the means, and that was okay, but anyone who said anything that had to do with my appearance was asking for a fight. My father was a pastor and he didn't manage his emotions, so why should I?

The first fight I got into at my new school was because of my eye. Supposedly one of the biggest, toughest kids was Little Anthony. He thought he was funny when he called me a "four-eyed, cockeyed boy, with big thick glasses!" in front of my peers. After school, I showed Little Anthony who a four-eyed cockeyed country boy was and I beat his tail real good! Little Anthony wasn't so big and bad after that. I didn't like fighting, but I set my mark with Little Anthony so the other kids would know what to expect. Doing so meant I wasn't exercising any discipline, which was part of my problem. I was making choices that appealed to self-gratification. When Mom found out about my fight with Little Anthony, her expression displayed her disappointment. "Life is not at the end of your knuckles," she warned. That was her way of suggesting I do a self-examination and reflect on my behavior. Who was I becoming? And why? The problem was that I no longer practiced the discipline I was raised to have, I wasn't submitting to God for guidance, and my choices were not aligned with the word of God. I blamed it on what happened and that our routine as a family was different. I wasn't walking into a house with the aroma of Grannie's mouthwatering fried chicken, boiled okra, rice, flavorful pinto beans and warm, sweet, buttery cornbread permeating my nostrils before I sat down for dinner. The promise of Grannie's banana pudding or caramel cake no longer existed and there weren't mandatory meals with Mom's brothers and Grannie. I didn't have my family to talk to about our day and no one was doing an integrity check on us. The only thing about dinner that remained the same was that Lloyde Johnson wasn't there.

When discipline goes out the window, other good habits are sure to follow. Fighting was one issue, and, given that I now had the options I always wanted, I decided I wasn't going to do schoolwork, so that became another.

Mom was eyeing me when I came in from school one afternoon without books in my hands and she stated, "You never have any books."

I shrugged.

"Why aren't you bringing them home?"

"Because I don't have any homework," I replied under my breath. She cut her eyes at me, grabbed her purse, and headed upstairs. My mother didn't believe me, but I knew she didn't have the time to do anything about it. Mom was headed to work her usual twelve-hour shift.

I wasn't taking my work seriously. What was I doing in that school anyway? I didn't want to be there. I thought it was temporary and we would eventually go back to Symonds. If we didn't go on our own accord, I thought Dad would come and get us—so I waited things out. A few months went by, then a few more, and a year passed. He never came.

Even though we lived with Aunt Doris, she was busy

with her family, so she didn't pay that much attention to us. Mom was working so hard to take care of us; she didn't notice I was slipping through the cracks right up under her nose. Before the disconnection of our family, my parents, Grannie, and uncles wouldn't have tolerated my behavior. We moved—they weren't there—and my gravitational pull was going toward being naughty. No one in St. Louis knew me. No one could tell Mom I was acting out. And I could keep secrets in that big city. I liked that.

It wasn't until I wanted to play football that I realized my choices had consequences. The football coach said that I couldn't play any sports until I improved my grades. When my English teacher Ms. Love spoke to Mom and told her, "Lekevie has potential," that resonated with me because I was on the cusp of not caring at all. Her statement made me look within myself and decide whether I wanted to do better because I knew I could. I thought football would help me focus on something I loved rather than what I was angry about. And it did. Gripping that cowhide football became my driving factor to work harder. Mom and Ms. Love collaborated to help me improve my grades by becoming disciplined in my study habits, more organized, and prepared for homework and tests. I committed to their process, worked hard, and my eligibility to play football was reinstated.

From the day Mom found Higher Heights, a church in St. Louis, she connected Frentrous and me to their men's group. That was her way of trying to give us the spiritual guidance she believed we needed. James Coleman ran the group. This guy was 5'2" at best, well-groomed, and when he spoke to me, he'd tuck his thumb under his index finger and point at me. Mr. Coleman had a good job, beautiful home, and a red hatchback Mercedes, but his spirit is what stood out the most. He didn't have any children, but he constantly invested in my brother and me. I thought Mr. Coleman saw Frentrous and me as two young men who needed to be put back on track, and I couldn't disagree. I knew the difference between right and wrong. I went off track because that's what I wanted. I had the freedom to figure out who I was and what I wanted to do, but what caused the deviation from who I was being raised to be was my anger. I was rich with anger, and that was separating me from God. I'd grown distant, picked up a little speed, and, before I knew it, I was running from God. I was the pendulum that swung in the opposite direction of everything I had learned. I didn't understand why everything that happened in my parents' life had to affect my life. I didn't do anything—but Dad was the preacher. He was supposed to be a good man and a leader. Instead, my father's selfish decisions had consequences that affected his family. His relationship with God wasn't enough. And, equally so, my mother made decisions that impacted us, too. The disconnection from my family made me want to disconnect from God.

We had been living in St. Louis for almost three years. Mom made sure we continued going to church, but I wasn't living that way—and I knew what was missing. I was raised in church and taught the Word of God from the beginning but, oddly, it was Mr. Coleman who felt there was something I needed to learn, and that was how to pray.

One afternoon, we were at our men's group. Mr. Coleman had all of us stand in a circle. He said he was going to teach us how to pray. I thought he was going to tell me something I already knew, only Mr. Coleman instructed us differently. "Just talk. Tell God how you feel—what you feel—and what it is you want Him to do," he said.

I did what Mr. Coleman told me to, and I spoke to God. For someone who had been running, I had a lot to say.

"God, I want to be in my own home. I want to have people and friends around us who care about us. And God, I really want to get back home to my grandmother," I added, trying not to sound as if I were pleading, but I was.

I was a pastor's kid. In my mind, I thought I had to approach prayer differently. I thought praying was something I had to be gifted with and that I needed to pray the way Grannie prayed. Since my father never taught me how to pray, I just recited Grannie's prayer. She'd say, "Father, here we come, humbled, eyes closed, head bowed, knee bent, and body bowed, your servant. We belong to you. You give us that which we need and we trust you for that. Thank you that the bed I slept in last night wasn't a cooling board, the sheets that covered me wasn't my winding sheet, the four corners of my walls were not the four corners of my grave. Amen."

I didn't know prayer was about God and I having a conversation, but I continued talking just the way Mr. Coleman instructed. The more I spoke to God, the better I felt about my life; and being connected to God helped me see my life coming together.

By high school, Mom acquired a better job and found a place for us to live. It was a two-bedroom apartment in a two-family flat. That red brick home needed a lot of improvements. Things were improving, and I started thinking about my future. My cousin Dannie played football at Sumner High School, and when he graduated, he played for Northern Iowa, which encouraged me to focus on football and cultivate my skills as a quarterback. I thought my work ethic and passion for football would create an opportunity to play in college, so I gave it everything I had.

Dad never called or came to visit us in St. Louis, so he couldn't see what I was trying to accomplish and how well I was doing. Eventually, I found out that my father had gone on with his life and married the woman from church. Mr. Coleman, Mom, and Ms. Love were in the stands one week after the other and it felt good to have their support.

My junior year, I became the starting quarterback for the Bulldogs. That's when a high level of arrogance kicked in. It just seemed to take over. Even though it wasn't necessary, I realized that my talent allowed me to manipulate the system in regard to schoolwork, so I did, and the consequences followed. Our team was out on the practice field running through new plays to catch the competition off guard. We were minutes away from boarding the two charter buses headed to Jefferson City when I saw Mom pull up in her Columbia blue Nissan station wagon. She got out of her car and started speed-walking toward us with Mr. Coleman trailing behind her. I thought something was wrong, so I headed in Mom's direction, but she brushed right past me with a paper in her hand. Mom wasn't there to see me. She was heading straight for Coach Walls. When I saw my mother showing my coach that paper, I knew it was my report card. I had a solid D in Geometry. Coach Walls waved me over. When I approached them, Coach Walls was mid-sentence pleading on my behalf, "Ms. Johnson, you can't do this. Give him another chance."

My coach didn't realize Mom wasn't listening. She didn't come to listen, and she never intended to have a discussion. Her mind was made up. I didn't know why Mr. Coleman had to tag along and bear witness to that; he didn't say a word in my defense. Mr. Coleman just studied my expression and listened to my coach. Coach Walls did his best to advocate for me to play that day, but in the end, he conceded and told me, "Your mom said you can't go."

That was the most important game of the year, and I thought my mother was the worst lady in the universe for making that one grade an issue on that day. I turned away from them and took off running. I thought I'd hide until she left with Mr. Coleman, then I'd sneak on the bus and deal with the consequences after the game. I clearly didn't think that plan through because Mr. Coleman found me hiding behind a building next to the field.

"Are you going to defy your mom?" he asked, pointing at me. I looked away without responding. "What is your decision going to be?" he questioned firmly.

There was nothing to say because I was disappointed in my actions. Mr. Coleman came there to hold me accountable for my behavior, and that caused me to take ownership of the situation I'd placed myself in. Mom had given me the green light to play football contingent upon my grades remaining acceptable, and they weren't. After making me look at what I was becoming and reflect on my core values, Mr. Coleman convinced me to get in the car and respect my mother's decision.

That night, I sat in my bed asking myself how I'd arrived at that place of making poor decisions. I had completely disregarded my upbringing. Why wasn't I taking responsibility for my behavior? More importantly, how could I turn things around? After having a conversation with myself, I had a new appreciation for Mom standing her ground. It wasn't that I couldn't do the schoolwork; I just wanted to circumvent the system because I had alternatives that allowed it. Short-term, I did what I wanted. Long-term, it hurt me. Late that night, Coach Walls and my cousin Little Danny stopped by our house with the team and handed me a medal. Our team won the state championship—without me.

By the middle of my junior year, I had turned things around again and my life was much better. I began taking responsibility for my behavior and said no to things that would keep me off track because my choices were aligned with the Word of God. The challenge I had with my education wasn't that I didn't have the ability to grasp what was being taught, it was my inability to be taught that created the problem. When I submitted to what was necessary and best for me, I began to excel in school again and compete at a higher level with football. Like my cousin Little Dannie, I planned on playing football in college. However, we never know when something will force us off the course we choose and onto the one God intended for us. My senior year, during a game against O'Fallon Tech, a heavy shot to my lower back by a linebacker brought an end to football. I spent time trying to fight through it, but I wasn't the same physically or emotionally. I loved the game and because of it, I lost something when it ended. Coach tried to give me things to do to contribute to the team, but my impact wasn't there. I was devastated. I'd felt lost for so long that when I finally found where I belonged—I thought it was on a football field.

When the problem begins, look within and do a self-examination:

1. Keep your emotions in check. You don't win on emotions; you win off hard work and discipline in your behaviors.

2. Know what drives you. Passion and preparation are connected.

3. Be organized. Organization is key in your life when you talk about improvement.

4. Who holds you accountable? Determine if you have anyone in your life that will tell you the truth about yourself. Make sure your network consists of individuals who will not compromise their integrity and are honest with you.

2.

WHO ARE YOU?

"And the Lord God formed man of the dust of the ground, and breathed into his nostrils the breath of life; and man became a living soul."

Genesis 2:7 (KJV)

~

After you have completed a clear self-examination, it is important to embrace what you have learned about who you are. This evaluation shouldn't be based upon the desire for self-gratification, but rather who God created. There are significant aspects that illustrate God's creations. He created humanity complete, He created humanity with value, and He created humanity with purpose. Embracing each of these is critical to staying on the course of spiritual success and productivity in life. The feeling of incompleteness is often brought on as a result of not knowing the value in what you possess.

When God created Adam and Eve, He made them complete. Everything they needed to produce was already inside of them. If they had embraced the value that comes with being complete, then the serpent has nothing to offer; but they did not. You must ask, Am I listening to something or someone because I feel like I'm not complete? Or am I listening because I don't know my true value? Too many times the appetite of humanity is enticed by things that sound good but are a total contradiction to the good that is already in you.

The serpent made its words sound tempting and presented them as something that was going to improve Adam and Eve. The reality is, when God created humanity, He had already declared that humanity was good. Nothing is more important than when God declares who you are. His declaration of who you are should serve as the driving force to denounce anything or anyone else that tries to define you. Adam and Eve had an opportunity to eliminate the serpent's definition of who they could be by embracing the declaration of what God had already concluded.

There will be moments in life when you will have to separate from anything and anyone who is looking to redefine you. There will be serpents disguised as people who will attempt to get you to step outside of who you are. These defining moments will show how rooted you are in your spiritual life, or you can take the path of Adam and Eve and pursue something that looks good, tastes good, but in the end is no good. The important lesson of who you are must be grounded and steadfast in what God has already declared.

You must remember your value. Looking at Adam and Eve illustrates how valuable they are to God and the environment in which they had been placed. They were responsible for everything. The major requirement for them was to obey His instructions and remain in the presence of God. These two requirements are spiritual. Anytime you get away from the spiritual being that God created, you diminish your value and who you really are. Your appreciation should drive your motivation to obey and stay in the presence of God.

Appreciation to God is a spiritual component that will keep you in His presence. Take a moment to reflect on your personal life. How many times have you found yourself unappreciative of what God has done for you? Do you value what you already possess, or are you searching for more? You cannot allow your relationship with God to falter. When it does, you are in the process of disconnecting, not only from who you are, but from your Creator. God was walking in the Garden looking for Adam and Eve, but He couldn't find them because they had stepped outside of who they were.

They were now able to see things that they had never seen, and they were faced with questions that they couldn't answer. Adam and Eve were embarrassed by what they had done and blamed each other for their current condition. Adam declared; it was the woman you gave me. Eve declared; it was the serpent. Individuals who don't take responsibility for who they are blame others, which is what I had been doing.

After graduating from high school in 1993, I hadn't considered anything beyond playing football in college. Due to my injury, that option was removed, and I was back at square one. I hadn't prepared to do anything else. Short of any other choices, I decided to join the Marines, the branch of the services with the reputation of being the hardest and toughest. I went to the recruiting office in North St. Louis County, Missouri and enlisted. After passing the physical and the Armed Services Vocational Aptitude Battery test, I was ready to serve.

I reached boot camp in San Diego, California and quickly realized that my recruiter Sgt. Cole had done nothing more than recruit me into a dream. I was about to learn the reason he insisted, "The quickest way through boot camp is graduation. Don't play hurt. Don't do anything." When we got off the plane, Marines were there to greet us. They were nice and said "Welcome, welcome" with friendly smiles as they directed us to the white buses that would take us to Marine Corps Recruit Depot, which was boot camp. The bus ride was surprisingly quiet. I don't recall hearing anyone engaged in a conversation, as if everyone was wondering, "What did we do?" When we reached the base, it seemed as though we had been recruited by Dr. Jekyll and sent to Mr. Hyde. I didn't know what to expect, but it wasn't a sergeant in a khaki short-sleeved shirt, green slacks, black patent leather shoes, and a round campaign hat yelling and screaming at the top of his lungs at the recruits. That sergeant positioned himself in the face of the recruits, the brim of his hat almost touching a recruit's forehead. It was a complete culture shock. Within 24 hours I realized the Marines planned to tell me what to wear, when to get up, when to go to bed, when to eat, and everything else.

The lessons were swift. Each morning—before making our beds or anything else—we were ordered to put on our green socks and black boots. Why? It was about protecting our feet. If we had to move in a hurry, we could do so. And it would prove necessary to be able to move around in all types of terrain. My first morning there, three drill sergeants made their statement by entering the barracks at 4 a.m. and banging on the beds, making as much noise as possible, screaming and yelling, "Get out of the rack! Get out of the rack!" Their goal was to create a chaotic environment to see if we would lose our discipline amid the chaos. They'd jolt our beds, shove stuff around, and do whatever else they could to rattle us. They were observing how fast we responded and whether we put our shirt or boots on first. They had to know. A lack of discipline could get someone hurt or killed because of a forgotten detail from training—and we practiced, all right. If someone got it wrong, we'd all return to bed and do it over and over again until we mastered it. If any of us didn't get it right, every one of us did push-ups.

One thing we practiced relentlessly was fire watch. Fully dressed, carrying our weapons and everything we were issued, we patrolled the perimeter for an hour and 20 minutes each night while everyone else slept. When done, we woke up our replacements. If we were in the mess hall, I had to put my hand over my coffee cup or soda cup and yell, "Gain way! Live grenade!" I was telling everyone to move aside. If I spilled anything, I blew everyone up, but I never spilled a drop. There was a process to follow, and valuable lessons every step of the way. The Marine Corps was preparing us for combat by instilling qualities that were necessary to survive. We needed to have consistent, positive habits because they are a part of life's plan. It didn't take long to be reminded that the concept of discipline through repetition worked.

During physical training, guys cracked under pressure. Some would ask to go to the restroom; when their request was ignored, they'd relieve themselves in their pants. I'd made up my mind that wasn't going to be me. I realized that the drill sergeants screamed and yelled every chance they had, but they didn't touch us. I had an option, and I took it. When I said, "Recruit Johnson requests permission to go to the restroom" and they ignored me, I stepped out of line and went anyway.

Of course, they didn't just let me walk away. Those drill sergeants followed me to the stall yelling and screaming, "You better not use it! You better not drop your pants!"

They screamed outside the stall and over the stall, but they never came in. After that bit of insubordination, I wasn't allowed to eat, but they did provide a nutritious drink as a replacement. As if that wasn't enough—they punished the whole platoon, too.

The recruits shouted "Thank you, Recruit Johnson" as they did push-ups, sit-ups, and wall sits while holding their weapons at arm's length with one hand.

I replied, "I didn't tell them to do this to you."

The sergeants wanted the platoon upset with me so they would police their own, but more importantly, they wanted us to work as a unit. That was a novel idea. Working as a unit produced more productivity and accountability.

While I was in boot camp, Mom held me accountable. She continually asked if I went to church, but I didn't have the heart to tell her that I was churched out. "No, Ma'am. I didn't get a chance to go this time." I always had some excuse. Amendment I of the U.S. Constitution carefully balances the protection of the free exercise of religion and protection from governmental establishment of religion. The Marines gave us time off for religion, but I was determined not to go to church. The irony was that some of the other recruits went because after they prayed, or if they weren't there to pray, that was a time to relax. The drill instructors couldn't be anywhere around recruits or in the building during church and chapel; they had their own time for that. Apparently, since football didn't work out, I chose to be a Marine. Even then, I was busy fighting my destiny. At boot camp graduation, Sergeant Horn told Mom and my girlfriend Rochelle, "He's stubborn. He had to do things his way. But he is a leader."

After boot camp, I was stationed in Okinawa, Japan, away from family, friends, morals, discipline, church, God—everything. Living the way I wanted was easy because there was no one holding me accountable in my personal life. I didn't have to look in the mirror, and I certainly wasn't looking within. I was frustrated that I made that alternative choice. Football had become my motivation for doing better, working harder in school, and trying to reconnect with God. I was doing the opposite of what I really wanted to do. Regardless of what I tried to accomplish, I kept seeing setbacks. I was still at the point of blaming my father. I hadn't embraced what I could learn or what would help me mature and grow. The outcome; I continually made everything someone else's fault, and that's why I was there. I was learning more about myself.

If we went against being anything other than who the Marines wanted us to be, they had ways to manage our behaviors. They docked our pay, placed us on restrictions, and implemented a host of other disciplinary actions. I typically left base on the weekends, but if I was on barracks restriction, I couldn't go anywhere. I tried to circumvent their system, but it didn't work. It took me two paychecks and two barrack restrictions to realize the Marines didn't provide the option to do things my way. They held me accountable for everything I did, and they had the brigs for anyone who refused to comply.

When I returned to Twentynine Palms, California, I was at a place where I understood that I was trying to do things my way rather than trusting God. I was still fighting the thought of going to church, reading my Bible, and talking to God. I was fairly certain that I was done with the whole religious, Christianity piece. I'd done that already, and I didn't think I needed it anymore. I was determined to do something completely different by focusing on maximizing my potential and building upon that growth. When I began following instructions, my career skyrocketed. There is something to be said about how important it is to follow God's instructions. I received a Meritorious Unit Commendation because I had become a poster Marine. As long as my way was working, I was comfortable doing it without God.

I had developed a passion for talking and interacting with people, and it felt natural. The Marines must have thought so, too, because they sent me back to St. Louis for six months to work with Sgt. Bowman as a recruiter; selling the same dream that Sgt. Cole sold me. I was 6'3", but small in frame at 145 pounds. Wearing my dress blues enhanced my self-esteem. Over a six-month period, I felt like a used car salesman— with people's lives. I was naturally skilled at talking to people and selling the Marines. During that period, I increased Sgt. Bowman's numbers and we exceeded our quota. I received a promotion to the rank of an E4, gained medals, and had 19 guys under me without reading my Bible, going to church, or developing a relationship with God. The core principals I learned in Symonds, Mississippi were displaced. I wasn't who God created. My time was spent working toward my own success rather than my spiritual success. I had already disconnected from God, which meant I was disconnected from who I was. I lived one way as a Marine and another when I was off duty.

One weekend, I got a pass and hightailed it to Vegas. The morning I was supposed to be back, I was a little late and tired, but I made it in line at 5:00 a.m. by rushing to get there, and that meant I skipped a step somewhere in the process. When you're living a double life, at some point, it overlaps. As soon as I got in line, there were approximately 40 guys locked in on me like I'd committed a major offense. I had no idea what their problem was because I was dressed in my PT clothes, but I became annoyed with their staring.

I shrugged my shoulders and snapped, "What? What are you looking at?"

One of them pointed to my ear and replied, "You have that earring in your ear."

While in high school, I had my ear pierced at the mall without my mother's permission. Living my double life, I had gone out that weekend wearing my silver hoop earring with a little rhinestone in it. One of my guys whispered "Johnson! Johnson! Kill the earring!" but it was too late. I was near the front row because I was an E3. I had to be in my proper place in line—hoop earring and all. The sergeant who led PT, my staff sergeant, and the gunnery sergeant over the entire platoon were all in front of me. The problem was Article 132, the Military Code of Uniform Justice. When PT was over, I was sent directly to the Staff Sergeant's office. Once he sent me to the lieutenant, I knew it was night, night. Not being definitive in upholding the Marine core values not only cost me a stripe, but also a level of pay that I'd worked hard to receive. In all of 30 minutes, I went from an E3 to an E2. I told him that I was sorry and the Lieutenant replied, "You can't be sorry in combat. There is no excuse for making this type of decision. If you are in combat and one of your fellow Marines gets killed, are you going to tell their mom or dad you're sorry that their son died?"

When you are undisciplined, the slightest wrong decision can get somebody killed in war. If you aren't dressed properly and out of uniform, the enemy can start counting from you because they can see the odd man out. That quick lesson, which derived from something as insignificant as an earring, created a major turning point. It forced me to evaluate the direction of my life by looking within to do a self-examination and asking myself, "Who are you?" I had to find out through my relationship with God because on my own, I didn't know who I was or my value.

The following Sunday, I was in California on a search to find a church. Even though I hadn't been going, I was still a church boy. I knew where the churches were. I found a white church with blue trim around the frame of the building that looked like the churches that I'd attended back in Symonds. For some reason, this particular church looked like it belonged out in the country—perhaps it found me. When I went inside and realized that it was a Baptist church, I stayed for the service. It wasn't as lively as my father's church, or the one my mother found in St. Louis, but the message was really good. I didn't make it that next Sunday, but I never missed another service the rest of my time in Twentynine Palms. I had neglected my faith, what I was reared to believe, and what I had already accepted. It was time to get back to my core principles and beliefs. I had strayed from that path for far too long. I wasn't running to God now that things were falling apart; I always knew I should never have disconnected in the first place. I thought I was enjoying life, but I'd failed at being disciplined while having fun. That is a principle we often get away from, especially when we are exploring.

If you don't ask yourself what your core principles are, you may not know. In fact, you may never know. Why does it matter? Knowing drives accountability. Once I mapped out what I was going to accomplish as a Marine, I vowed not to fight against military protocol or entertain negative influences. My entire approach and attitude changed because not only were they holding me accountable for my actions, I elected to start holding myself accountable. It wasn't until then that it all worked out. After six years of service in the Marines Corps, I learned that when there is no discipline, destruction is certain to follow.

Getting back to my faith was critical for me. I was certain that the absence of God was going to lead me to an uncomfortable life. Everything I was doing outside of the will of God was forced; there was nothing natural about it. I was angry, annoyed, and upset with my father. In essence, I was taking all of the pieces of the puzzle of my life and trying to make them fit, and to do it, I kept bending the pieces.

I needed to reach the point where my life was less complicated and smoother because I was no longer self-sabotaging. I knew there would be hurdles, as that's a part of life. The issue was that I created those hurdles. I was fighting against my destiny, which is the reason I continually created a sundry of obstacles; I wasn't on my charted course. I was trying to complete myself my way instead of embracing the declaration of what God had concluded. I discovered that options are great, but they will expose who you are, just as they did me. Ask yourself, what am I drawn to now? Do those things support what I believe? When I have people who are beneficial to me, why am I drawn to those who are not?

When Adam and Eve ate the forbidden fruit from the Tree of Knowledge after God told them not to, it exposed who they were. They had so many other alternatives in the garden, but for some reason, there was an appetite that went beyond what they already possessed—and it tore our world apart. My father's appetite did the same with our family, and my appetite was in the process of doing the same in my life.

I had gone to see Grannie while I was in the Marines, and she was so proud of me. It had been a few years, so I felt I needed to go back. Whenever I went to see her, Grannie wanted me in my uniform, so I'd pack it just for her. I didn't get to see her very long, but I made that seven-hour drive to see her in Mississippi after seeing Mom. I didn't look for Dad even though I drove right through his town. Not being able to see Grannie as much as I wanted hurt me, but I couldn't go without calling her regularly, and she loved talking on the phone. Grannie wanted to know everything that was going on in my life. Everyone in the family knew Grannie sure loved me something special. She made me think of and examine the good parts of my life.

Self-examination helped me arrive at the place I was

supposed to be, and I understood where my connections were off. I knew I wasn't going to stay in the Marines. I finally accepted that I'd been called to do something different. I'd grown tired of fighting my destiny, and I didn't like the way it made me feel on the inside. I readjusted and charted a different path after my military career ended. With discipline, drive, and passion, I left the Marines an E5 and returned to St. Louis to accept my call to preach. God had already decided who I was going to be. That pull on my life was relentless, which is the reason I tried not to spend as much time with God. I wasn't ready. I kept busy with the other options; nonetheless, I knew that running wasn't going to last. Before I made another move, I needed to know who I was. I realized that I didn't want to be who I was apart from God.

Look within and ask yourself who you are. There are four important life principles in embracing who you are:

1. Be aware of any words that attempt to redefine you.

2. Be aware of any voice that contradicts the Word of God.

3. Appreciation keeps you aligned and obedient to His will and in the presence of God. You are God's most prized creation who possesses a great deal of value. Choose to live a life of appreciation.

4. Pay attention to how you feel on the inside when you make poor decisions.

3.

ARE YOU SATISFIED WITH YOU?

"For I know the thoughts that I have toward you, saith the Lord, thoughts of peace and not of evil, to give you an expected end."

Jeremiah 29:11 (KJV)

~

When God sees humanity, He immediately sees His thoughts. This thought is something that humans should use to arrive at the place of being satisfied with themselves. Perhaps this is an issue that our current society should evaluate. If the only time you are strong is when you utilize your power to disrupt the peace of others, it puts your weakness on display. The serpent had one objective—to birth chaos. Being satisfied with you is being satisfied with who God created. God has granted talents, gifts, and uniqueness to us; however, these are not the things that should be the foundation of being satisfied with who we are. It is important to remove from the equation talents, gifts, and uniqueness and focus on God's intention for creating you; it is in this place that satisfaction must be discovered. The challenge that we face is aligning our thoughts with God's thoughts. In order to be satisfied with who we are, there must be a shift in thoughts. How this shift takes place is accepting how God views humanity. His view of us is clearly outlined in the sacred text of the Bible. God's desire for us is to find satisfaction in the peace that He has given unto humanity. When we understand inner peace is at the core of satisfaction, then we will protect and eliminate anything that attempts to be a peace disturber. When humanity is at peace—satisfaction with self is inevitable.

When we are satisfied with who we are, it is easier to pursue our goals and to identify our potential. This is the issue that I faced when my peace was disturbed by the move Mom had to make when she was running to safety. I spent so much time trying to be unproductive because I wasn't functioning in a place of peace or satisfaction. Discovering my potential was the last thing on my agenda. I wanted to do things my way and stay away from doing things God's way. My stubbornness and lack of zeal for God was a sure sign that I was not satisfied with me. This is something that the serpent was able to expose in Eve and Adam. It should have been inner peace or satisfaction that motivated Eve and Adam to say no to the serpent. The serpent was a tenant in the garden, so it knew that the garden was a place of peace. The influence of the serpent exposed the weakness of Eve and Adam. There is nothing wrong with having a weakness; however, it is dangerous to make decisions from the place of weakness. Life's best decisions are made from the place of satisfaction. It is from that place that "no" is an asset to your vocabulary. Saying no can keep you on the path to accomplishing your goals. The serpent was able to keep

Eve and Adam from accomplishing the goals and assignment that God had given them.

The reality is harsh, but the truth is, Adam and Eve should have said yes to their Creator and no to the serpent. The minute they ate from the forbidden place, they said no to God and yes to the serpent. They opened the doors wide to having their peace disturbed. Being satisfied with you is accepting that you have weakness and strengths. They are both a critical part of your success. This is based on what the Bible has to say concerning your weakness. God allows our weakness so we can depend on His strength. This wisdom is recorded in 2 Corinthians 12:9. Humanity must embrace the fact that their greatest strength is in God. He is the one that drives humanity to the satisfied place. If God is absent from the life of humanity, so is the ability to be satisfied. The question, Are you satisfied with you? can be answered based upon humanity's decision to tell God yes. This is something I learned the hard way, and there is no reason for you to learn the same lesson.

Eve and Adam teach humanity the reason why saying no is important and why functioning from a place of peace is critical to life decisions. Being aware of anything or anyone who wants to disturb your peace is a great attribute to have.

When I returned to St. Louis, I stayed with Mom for a month and then I found my own two-bedroom condo. It was in South St. Louis. Given my military background, the Adams Mark Hotel hired me as their Director of Security. My co-workers, the clientele, and celebrities that I had the opportunity to meet kept it interesting and fun. Frentrous was the overnight auditor, and he recommended that I apply. My brother was doing well in the hotel industry, although it wasn't what I wanted to do. After being in the military, I knew I wasn't where I needed to be. The job paid decent money, but internally, I was missing some pieces and I needed to detox. In reality, I was still attempting to function without my full connection to God. I was trying not to follow in anyone's path, especially Lloyde Johnson's. I knew I was making decisions that were not aligned with the spiritual person, the calling God placed in my life, and it weighed heavily on me. I didn't want to go to church and talk to God. It was frustrating enough to choose a church I should go to, especially after the optics I had seen. I used my history—in essence, everything that my father had done— as my excuse to remain in the comfort zone. As long as I could focus on Dad, it wasn't hard for me to do better than what he had done. He was my measuring tool, and I didn't have much to measure. As I said, I was comfortable. I wasn't manipulating, abusing, or hurting people. However, time taught me that I was hurting myself because I wasn't reaching my full potential. Admittedly, I shared some of my father's tendencies, one of which was doing things differently.

When we make choices, we often know precisely why we make them. We know what we are trying to do or avoid and the reason behind it. I didn't like that I wasn't fully committed yet, which led me to take the time to have a little self-talk. The first question I asked myself was why I was still running from my destiny. I had the resources to help me get back on track, and that self-talk inspired me to reconnect with James Coleman and Higher Heights. It was there that I stopped fighting it and accepted my call to ministry. Initially, I did not discuss my intentions with the pastor; instead, I got in my car and drove to Symonds to see my father.

On that trip, I had seven hours to think about everything I wanted to tell Dad. It wasn't until my military service was nearly over that I sent my father a picture of me in uniform. He may not have cared, but I wanted him to know that I was doing something with my life and making something of myself without him. I was angry when I picked up the pen and wrote on the back, "It's me, all is well." I thought about having graduated without any connection with my father at all. He wasn't the best person to have in my life, but he was my father, and he was my pastor for the first twelve years of my life. After we left Symonds, Dad never called me, and he didn't come to St. Louis while Mom was struggling to raise us on her own. When I finished bootcamp, the only people that came to my graduation were Mom and Rochelle. I'm not sure why I expected Dad to be someone he simply wasn't and actually care, but I just wanted him to be my father. For some reason, I found it hard to let go of that dream, while in reality, many years had passed without speaking to my biological father, the pastor.

My head held so many thoughts, and my heart harbored a great deal of hurt. I wanted Dad to know that, somehow, I was going to be so much better than him. My intentions and motivations would not be to use or mislead a congregation for the purpose of entertainment or financial gain. It would not be to deceive them. I was going to lead by example and let the Word of God be my guide.

When I arrived in Symonds, I found that Dad had moved and remarried without so much as letting me know. The only way I could find him was to retrieve his address from one of my uncles. His new address was 625 Page Street in Clarksdale, so I went there. When I knocked on the door of his double-wide trailer, the lady he cheated on while he was married to Mom answered the door. I wasn't surprised to see her, and she knew who I was. The fact that my father had been absent from our lives made it evident that he had moved on with his.

"Is my dad here?"

"No," she replied sheepishly. Her former arrogant demeanor was no longer present. She looked like someone who hadn't survived the wrath of my father. Slow movements and wrinkles under her eyes had replaced youth and vibrancy. "You can come in. I can call him at work," she offered. She went into the kitchen and called my father at Clarksdale Public Utilities. I felt uncomfortable being there, and as soon as she told me where to meet him, I left.

Dad pulled up at Double Quick wearing a blue Clarksdale Public Utilities ballcap. When he got out of his white work truck, he was wearing a white work shirt and black dress pants with a ring of keys hanging on the side of his hip. Dad was a petite man and had aged. His face was wrinkled, and I could tell the stress had consumed him. He already had a dark complexion, but now he seemed darker. He had on a pair of gold-framed glasses that he probably bought off the rack at Fred's dollar store. It had been 12 years since I'd seen him. We shook hands and walked into the convenience store.

It was a bit awkward, but I'd gone there to tell him something I needed him to know, so I went straight to the point of my visit and said, "Hey, I wanted you to know that God has called me to preach." I was waiting for him to ask why, whether I was sure, or what I had done over the years to reach this conclusion.

He said, "I always knew that you would be a preacher. How long are you in town?"

"Not long, I'm going out to the country to see my folks and then I'm leaving."

I don't know why I expected something more.

We sat down at a table for a few minutes. Everything about my disposition and communication told my dad that my intent was not to be anything like him. I wasn't confrontational with my father, even though it was my desire to understand why he abandoned us. The only reason I refrained from asking was that I had accomplished what I'd come there to do. I wanted him to sense that his son had grasped onto life even though he tried to destroy it. He wasn't powerful enough to stop God's plan. I had a brand-new black Chevy Beretta, and I didn't have to call him to work on it. I didn't need Dad for anything, but I wanted him to sense that every obstacle he put in front of Mom, my brother, and me did not put us in a bad place as he may have expected. I was going to accept the calling of God in his absence. He did it in our presence, but we were not engaged in the journey; we were the hindrance to his journey.

I just wanted him to look at me and realize that his son had turned out just fine with Mom raising me, Mr. Coleman guiding me, and the path I chose as a Marine. Other than creating me, my father couldn't take credit for anything I had accomplished. I couldn't help but think about how far and fast I'd run from God and the reasons why. My father had initiated the removal of my desire to accept the call God placed on my life. He caused me to believe that I didn't need God because of what he demonstrated and who he was as a man and a father. When I looked at him, it made me ask myself, What does hate look like? Does it make you stay away from your children? Does it make you drive 7 hours to say, Look at me, I'm still here? He never came to see me play football in high school, and boot camp was supposed to be the hardest thing I'd done in my life. I was a United States Marine, and he didn't know anything about me. How can you not care? He didn't show up for anything, but this time, I felt it necessary to go back to Symonds and show him. It wasn't that I wanted my father to be proud of me; he wasn't qualified to be proud of me.

I sat there with nothing more to say and his conversation was limited because he didn't know me. The only thing he could do was look at me and see what he missed out on. He couldn't even take credit as a pastor for teaching me how to talk to God.

We could have had a spiritual conversation, and I hoped he'd have some questions or curiosity about his son. He could have asked about my time in the military, my career, if I was sure about my decision, or why I was making it, but instead he repeated his previous question, "When are you going back?" It seemed as if he wanted to just get back to work. He'd been an absentee father for so long that he didn't have any idea what I'd done with my life. Furthermore, I had to find him. The only thing I knew at that point was that I didn't love him.

I sat there for 12-13 minutes with my father—at most. It was evident that my father's personality hadn't changed; he was always trying to move and be gone. Everything in life was more important than his family. He didn't make time for me. When I glanced out the window, I could see another guy sitting in his work truck waiting on him. Dad said he had to place an order for himself and the guy in the truck. Apparently, he'd asked the guy if he wanted some chicken, but he didn't ask me.

I watched my Dad get up and walk over to the counter to place his order. Physically, he looked as if his lifestyle had taken its toll. He moved like he was aging aggressively. Dad grabbed his chicken and left. I headed to the Delta to see my real folks. I was satisfied that I saw my father. It was clear that I was not him.

I had been dating Rochelle since high school. When I went into the military, we stayed in touch. Rochelle had a small frame and was always well-dressed, with a short, layered haircut. Her smile could illuminate any room. She was comfortable in her skin and she was sexy. When I returned, she was working at Maritz's Marketing firm and transitioned to working with juveniles in a rehab center.

I returned and told the Bishop I was accepting my call to preach. Training was an imperative part of his process, and I thought he was a phenomenal teacher. He mentored me for preparation for the first sermon. I wasn't content with being at the Adam's Mark because I felt I was meant to do something more. There was a guy I met through church; he was a preacher and he owned a mortgage company. I had known him for a number of years. He was recruiting people for his company, and he sold me on it. It was commission-based, and I was paid every two weeks at the Adam's Mark. From that aspect, I was doing well and was happy with my life. At the age of 24, I was preparing for my first sermon, Stay Focused, referencing I Thessalonian 5:16-20. I had twenty minutes to preach, and Rochelle's mom hired a videographer to capture that moment. The reality is that I was preaching to myself. Everything I preached started with me. That is one of my best attributes. If I don't do it, I feel that I am not qualified to tell other people to do it. I chose it because I needed to stay focused. It can be easy to develop a high level of arrogance when preaching because people cater to preachers.

I was satisfied with my financial stability. I had found a balance between working at Adam's Mark and the mortgage company. While I was involved in my church, Rochelle continued attending her home church. She was a youth director, and she was genuinely engaged there. Her sister, cousin, and a friend had a singing group; they were one of the most talented groups I'd ever heard. It was outside of me the level of talent they had. They were content with being a local phenomenon rather than being a global success.

I was beginning to develop a mindset of what success looked like spiritually. I considered my next steps and where I was going.

One morning, Rochelle asked me to pick up some dry cleaning for her. It presented the perfect opportunity since I had planned on going to Helzberg to purchase a platinum ring I had previously selected. When I arrived at the juvenile center, Rochelle looked at me as if she were wondering why I brought her dry cleaning to her job. I laid her dry cleaning on a counter and dropped to one knee. She quickly said, "No! No! No! Let's go in here." She pulled me off my knee and I followed her into an office. I proceeded to propose to Rochelle, my high school sweetheart. After she said yes, she called her mom, Flora, while I called Mom and then Grannie.

I made enough money to purchase some real estate and start my own mortgage company. I hired my brother, his wife, and Mom, and Rochelle left her company to help me build Unlimited Mortgage. I was in a good spiritual place and felt God was doing something in my life.

In 1999, our church was preparing for a live recording for our choir co-produced by Bishop Hawkins, who produced and collaborated on numerous hit songs listed on the Billboard Gospel Music charts. The plan was to tour the East Coast to promote it. My brother came to me and recommended that I invest in underwriting the tour. As a 24-year-old, I entered into an agreement with my Bishop and his partner. At the time, it seemed as though it made sense because it was a short-term investment and I was singing and playing the drums in our choir.

When I spoke with my attorney at the time, Gaylord Williams, he warned, "I know this is the church, but let's be wise in case push comes to shove."

Given the agreement was with my church, my Bishop, and my brother had brought it to me, I said, "No, I think I'm alright." But still, Gaylord insisted to a deaf ear.

We met in the Bishop's office at our church with the Deacons and trustees present. They asked me for the money, and they agreed, in writing, to pay me back. I signed the unsound agreement after being told that my investment would be repaid when the week-long tour was complete. They expected to profit from the tour. The first cashier's check I handed them was $13,600. Prior to leaving for the tour, I gave them the next payment of $10,000 as an investment to cover expenses, and the final investment was paid close to the end of the tour for $17,000. It didn't register that I should have questioned what they expected their return to be and when they would start making money.

The agreement stated I was giving the production company an investment for our church tour and CD release. Bishop's signature was on the agreement. Given this was my church family, I didn't see the red flag when Bishop and his alleged partner had me make the check out to some production company rather than our church or the individual who signed the agreement—my Bishop. I questioned why the cashier's check and contract were not in the name of our church, as I was told. Bishop claimed the production company was governed by the church. Since it wasn't clarified that my investment was a loan in the agreement, I wrote "Loan" on the memo line of the cashier's checks. After the tour, I asked for my money, but Bishop claimed I had given them an offering.

It didn't take long before I found myself right back in nasty church stuff. I was the son of a pastor. I'd been an active part of church and was trained in churches. I knew what church looked like and what it should have been like. The church had a high level of dysfunction that hindered the ability to do ministry effectively. I had been in the inner circles and dwellings of church from childhood to adulthood and it had not deterred me from knowing what I was called to do. There had to be a generation that cared enough to help fix this. Until we told the truth and unmasked what was causing the dysfunction, how could we fix it or agree upon a resolution?

We had to go deeper to look within. There can be an ugly side to church, which is one of the reasons some people get what they can get from church and leave; they solely attend for the message. They don't want to be involved in the inner workings. My thoughts drifted back to history, reminding me how I felt with Mom and Dad. I contemplated whether I wanted to be connected to this.

I reached a fork in the road. Mom, Frentrous, and I attended the same church, and now, I was asking Rochelle to leave her church knowing that I was impacting her spiritual path. She grew up in her church, but she left and came to be at my church even though I was on the verge of deciding whether or not I was going to stay. That wasn't considerate on my part and proved that I was still in the process of my spiritual growth and maturity. It wasn't long before things got bad.

Our church was thriving in St. Louis. My brother was serving as Bishop's Adjutant. Although I could sense the shift in the relationships and environment, I couldn't stop what was already in motion. Allowing the external influences to impact life-long decisions is something that was going to be the challenge for me. I was experiencing external negative impact on family members, a lack of integrity from a leader we trusted, and a lack of commitment from a leader of parishioners to be open, honest, and transparent. This is not how church should be. I was impacted externally because I was beginning to remember and reflect on the reasons I didn't want to take that route and why I did everything in the military to avoid it. I was challenged with asking myself if I was sure this path was for me. I had my own personal relationship with God, and my frustration with the external stuff was affecting me, but I couldn't let it take me back to driving so far away from God who created me. When you are called upon and sure of the plan God has for your life, you cannot give your attention to the external elements around you because they will cause you to question why you are connected to them. There has to be balance. Whose voice is more important? The fact that God already has declared what you are going to be, or are you so caught up in what you see that now you are unsure about what God has spoken?

Go back to the garden. God had already spoken and given out assignments, He told Adam and Eve what they were going to be. Now, serpents traveled on this journey, and they also travel in the church. What better place to disrupt the satisfaction of humanity than to come into the territory that God has blessed them with? At times, we fail to understand that churches are filled with human beings who have different ideologies, philosophies, cultures, and upbringings. We need to embrace the governing authority, as there was in the garden, which is what God has said. What God says always governs the way of God.

The serpent's responsibility was getting humanity to disconnect from God's governing way and His word. The serpent's play on words deceived Eve, leading her to question God. She should have been asking herself the same question I had to ask myself: Is this who you want to be? The serpent seeks out weaknesses in humanity, which causes us to question God.

Knowing that my agreement with the church was not upheld and that I was not compensated when the tour ended, rather than right the wrong, Bishop was strategic in using the situation to divide and conquer our family. Now, a family cannot be divided if it isn't already fractured. Somewhere, we had a fracture that didn't reveal itself until then. Because of what we'd been through together, me, my mom, and brother were tight. Things didn't change between us until money came into play. The root of evil reveals a lot of truth. Bishop drove a wedge, pitting Mom and me against my brother—her eldest son. I wasn't happy with anything that was transpiring and, ultimately, my brother stopped talking to us. Mom walked down a side aisle in church one morning and I noticed Frentrous wouldn't acknowledge her presence. The look on my mother's face conveyed her devastation. Seeing the pain it caused Mom, who'd sacrificed everything for our physical, mental, and spiritual well-being, caused me to step away from what I was learning because it was in an environment that supported this type of con, anger, lack of faith, and disrespect. To find myself ready to fight my brother in the church parking lot felt reminiscent of when Dad hit my mother at church. He embarrassed her to a high level and seemed to think nothing of it. I took a brief moment, and asked myself one question: "Are you getting ready to repeat a cycle?" All of the things we saw with our father had both consciously and subconsciously impacted us. We were his children. He was our example. The gift of free will to behave like our father was our choice; no one else's.

It was an ugly scene that should never have happened. The church environment should not have condoned any division of family or church members. Commitments and contractual agreements should have been instinctive to honor. A matter of one's integrity and character. Why wasn't it?

When the rehearsal to follow Dad's steps began, Mom was pulling on my arm, crying and begging for me to let it go. Onlookers surrounded us and no one, as with my father, made any attempt to stop us. Everyone on that main street could see all of the raucous taking place. I was angry because Mom wasn't able to conceal the heartache we had caused, and she was hurting in a place —all over again—that should have facilitated healing. I think this time, with her two sons, it may have been worse. I don't think she expected anything of Dad, but she did expect more from us. We knew better because we were raised better. I was not satisfied with my behavior. I was not pleased with the outcome. I never intended to have this kind of anger toward my brother. What were we learning? Better yet, what were we becoming?

The serpent was speaking louder than anyone else, and we were listening. I wanted to follow the protocol that God put into place, but I was doing the opposite of what God was telling me. We were supposed to live under a new authority, and our relationship with God was supposed to govern us. Our lives were starting to mirror what we had been through before. The Bishop let my brother think Mom and I didn't have his vision. He sent my brother to ask me for the money to benefit the church, knowing my heart. The objective that the Bishop had when he did not want to hold his end of the contract was to divide and conquer. Bishop didn't call or reach out to try to mediate or do what a pastor should do and help us reconcile, especially for a family that had experienced fragmentation before. I was picking up on how church should look, and this wasn't it. Things can happen around you, but they should not change the course that God has put you on.

Church should place emphasis on impacting the heart of man. When individuals improve, the church improves. We are so busy trying to separate the structure and the organization from the people who are engaged and involved with it that we keep missing the mark every time. We have to start with the people rather than the structure or organization. The people either make the church progress or they keep it stagnant. A church cannot be built without the individuals who decided to engage themselves. While the garden was established, there was no productivity, multiplication, increase or maintenance if Adam and Eve weren't functioning properly. They had to be productive. This is not about you and your agenda; this is about Christ and His agenda. The serpent was the gates of Hell coming to change the agenda. The serpent can't change who we are, but it can influence us to make a decision that is contradictory to who we are—external measures. That is the challenge that the church faces, and what we must talk about. What are we building? And we must do so without playing the blame game. The negative stuff is so obvious, but shifting into a high level of positivity will cause negative people to either pack their bags and go or shift to the direction of the culture. If you constantly give negative situations a platform and the serpent your attention, that's who will govern the way.

The building we purchased on Olive St. Road was an old movie theatre turned into a church. It was the Bishop's church. When the leadership split, bad business decisions ensued and he had to sell the building. Bishop told his congregation they would buy a building. However, his infrastructure no longer existed. The assistant pastor tried to help get my money returned to me but was unsuccessful. Eventually, he moved on from the internal conflict and started his own church.

Sometimes, things happen that remind you of past experiences. Grandfather was separated from Grannie and he had another piece of property that he lived on.

My grandfather would borrow money from Mr. Bill and if he didn't pay it back, Mr. Bill took money out of everyone's pay connected to Grandfather. And as an insult, Mr. Bill gave us change as opposed to dollar bills. I believed that was his way of saying, "Your grandfather has already borrowed against your money. Here's what's left." I was supposed to get fifty to sixty dollars but didn't. Grandfather's actions impacted those connected to him. My father's actions impacted those connected to him. I was on the path to do the same as though it were a generational curse—and I had to break it.

I couldn't help but wonder if my grandfather and father were satisfied with who they were, which caused me to question myself. The answer was no. I knew better, so I had to do better in the eyes of God.

1. When you know who you are in God, satisfaction must be driven from that place.

2. Satisfaction comes as a result of finding inner peace and not external gain.

3. When you are satisfied with who you are, your ability to see distractions are heightened.

4. Do not allow anger or hate to become a distraction to who you are meant to be.

4.

SELF-TALK

"Take fast hold of instruction; let her not go: keep her; for she is thy life."

Proverbs 4:13 (KJV)

~

The idea surrounding self-talk is critical for staying in a place of constant improvement. It is vital to remain satisfied with yourself. What's significant is defining what self-talk is. Self-talk is consistently speaking the truth of what the Word of God has to say concerning his plan for your life. This definition takes the self-talk concept from words to actions. In order to accomplish self-talk, there must be motivation to read the word and seek out how to apply it to your life. This seems like a path that is easier said than done. God created humanity for the purpose of being connected to Him. This is done by following the principles that are outlined in His word. Knowing what the word has concluded concerning humanity is the first step in self-talk. It is impossible to speak what you don't know.

A good place to start is in the Garden of Eden. It is there that God gives humanity the tools for success and His words to remember. God created man in His image, blessed them, and gave them the natural ability to produce. God gave humanity power, clear instructions on what to refrain from, and the ability to make decisions. God was so kind to humanity that he gave them permission with parameters. It is important to know what you have permission for and where the parameters are. Compare the list of all that God gave to Adam and Eve and then look at what he did not give them permission to do. You would think that they would have been so busy with all they had, that they wouldn't have time to focus on what they couldn't have. Therefore, self-talk is important because it's a constant reminder of what God has given and what God has said. Even the serpent knew the parameters God had given to Adam and Eve. He used what God said and placed doubt in the mind of Eve. This guided Eve to make a bad decision. Self-talk would have led Eve on the path of declaring no to the serpent! This must be utilized as the mental driving force that helps maintain momentum. The absence of self-talk proved that the serpent's voice was able to silence their inner knowledge.

During my military career, I failed to remind myself that my actions shouldn't contradict my beliefs. I knew that God had a calling on my life, yet I ignored it to feed the natural man. Self-talk is all designed to get you to turn away from anything or anyone who is trying to get you to move in the opposite direction of your place of being productive.

Self-talk should also drive you to the place of constant communication with God. Yes, prayer is a critical piece, as the lack of prayer is the lack of power. The lack of power is the lack of productivity, which will hinder you from your divine purpose. When the serpent starts talking, you should start praying and stop listening. It will fuel the power that you have within and cause you to resist the external forces that are attempting to push you to the forbidden place. One visit to the forbidden place can cause chaos and disrupt your peaceful place. Being misled can come as a result of listening to the wrong voice, the biggest voice in your life must be the Word of God. It offers a 100% success rate. This is what God guarantees with His word. "For as the rain cometh down, and the snow from heaven, and returneth not thither, but watereth the earth, and maketh it bring forth and bud, that it may give seed to the sower, and bread to the eater: So shall my word be that goeth forth out of my mouth: it shall not return unto me void, but it shall accomplish that which I please, and it shall prosper in the thing whereto I sent it" (Isaiah 55:10-11 KJV). When you have the Word of God on the inside of you, it eliminates ineffectiveness, it causes growth, it drives productivity, and causes prosperity. This is one of the critical reasons self-talk must include rehearsing and repeating what the word has concluded.

I made the terrible mistake of disconnecting from my faith because I didn't view it from the lens of the Word of God but the actions of my father. I was so caught up in his actions that my faith was dwindling with my fiery determination not to be what I saw. Yet my actions were contradictory to the Word of God, which is why I was having fun while traveling an unproductive route.

Graduating from boot camp was the first biggest moment of my life. Accepting my call to ministry was the second. Preaching my first sermon in 1998 with Mom, Rochelle, Grannie, and all of Rochelle's family was third. On August 4, 2000, all of my uncles, my family, Rochelle's sister, the whole crew was there to witness our marriage, the next beautiful event of my life. Grannie and my uncles stopped in Clarksdale and even picked up my father. Rochelle and I had an incredibly beautiful wedding.

I had pursued the path to be a pastor since my early upbringing. I knew there was a call on my life to function as a Christian. I wasn't a kid who hated going to church, I enjoyed it. The manner in which people responded to my father was unbelievable and it piqued my interest. I wondered what would have happened if his intent was genuine and he had passion for ministering; he could have influenced even more people. The thought of being able to positively impact people made me want to pursue this path. I had something to offer because it was rooted in me—God put it there.

I had a million questions about religion and faith. I wanted to know what the Bible entailed, who wrote it, where it came from, the historical significance, and why people read and quoted it. I had a genuine interest in getting to the root of each question as I deemed that's where the truth was. I wanted to possess an elevated level of confidence, and the way to do it was understanding His word and precisely why I believed in God. That drove me. I was engaged in learning more by studying scripture. It helped me develop into the person I am today.

I didn't want the emptiness of claiming to believe and live by the word while betrothed in a life of hypocrisy. Watching Grannie's genuineness in her faith taught me more than what I saw from my father. By uprooting us from Symonds, Mom taught me the same. She changed the landscape and began building a foundation away from the toxicity. Her first piece of business was getting us back to church to continue building our relationship with God. I wondered what her motivating factor was for putting us back in church. Our church and the environment were not beneficial to her. It was toxic. I came to discover that church was her sanctuary. It was where her strength was derived. Mom had a place where she could cast her cares and stay focused on her journey.

My mother taught me that God reveals himself through His word. The absence of His word meant not having a relationship with Him. I had to ignore people who claimed they had a relationship with God but were without evidence that they did. If I focused on all the external occurrences of what the Christian faith looked like from my lens, I never would have taken that path. I had every reason to stay away from the Bible, prayer, and faith because I had a bad taste in my mouth; yet, I was still interested beyond those external factors which suggested that I had a genuine interest. There had to be a divine calling.

Having self-talk was a driving force for me then, and it's a driving force in my life today. Look around! We need it as a reminder that we know better. The best way to start is by acknowledging what is right and wrong and then fervently pursuing what is right. Let that be the reoccurring theme in your thought pattern. I simply ask myself, Lekevie, is it right or is it wrong? There is no doubt in my mind that my father never had that conversation with himself, which made me certain that it needed to be my starting place, which has become my life's theme. There is a fundamental difference between right or wrong and it can be measured. Just ask yourself if you can align what you are doing with what you have rehearsed through the Word of God. The absence of having a standard can be problematic. Once you set standards, ask yourself how you are going to reach and sustain them. Allow self-talk to become a constant reminder. If you pause long enough to simply ask yourself the qualifying question of whether or not something is right or wrong, your decisions will be better. You can talk about doing the right thing, but when it comes down to it, what are you going to do? What is convenient or easy isn't necessarily what is best. Saying no and making good decisions will become easier when you have self-talk and your actions reflect your answer.

Self-talk has become instinctive because I am married to it. I practice it, and it is now part of my foundation. I saw this was necessary by observing my father. It wasn't something he appeared to do. Had he practiced it, abusing and neglecting a family may never have occurred. He would not have needed to question whether it was right or wrong, and the negative or toxic things that happened may not have. If we don't talk to ourselves, we put ourselves in a position for everyone else to talk to us, which is what caused the chaos in the garden. What if Eve had rehearsed the question of foundation, is it right or wrong? Whose standard is it? Is this God's standard? Am I trying to reach a standard of something I was not designed to have? Why do you think you need this? Whose voice is the loudest? That voice is going to prompt the answer. Asking yourself qualifying questions that help you get to the root of why you want to do something and whether you should do it is how you look within. Answer the question then follow up by asking yourself: What am I going to do? At some point, the practice of self-talk creates a healthier habit when you review your track record.

A conversation with yourself will drive you to a good decision; it has to be a part of your norm. When you ignore the voice of God and have a conversation with the serpent, you are inviting chaos into your life. If you silence yourself, things are probably not going to work out so well. I didn't make great choices, but when I started having self-talk, I was aligning my decisions with what the word has to say. It was paramount for me to consider that. For so many years, I allowed situations or things to make me angry and shut down. I was impacted by an environment that was void of peace. Self-talk drove me away from that place of anger, and when you leave it, you realize that there is no viable reason to return.

I shared the barracks with a guy named Henderson who wore his Levi's so tight you could see the Copenhagen in his pocket. When we sat down to a meal, it was annoying because even with his mouth closed, he chewed ridiculously loud. Henderson's chewing got me to the point that I didn't like him anymore. It made me so angry that I had to ask myself why, because that was just how he ate. There are probably things he didn't like about me. I talked myself out of being irritated. I couldn't go through life nitpicking on things. That wasn't the person I aspired to be, and it was nothing other than a huge distraction to my progress and purpose. What's on the inside of you determines how you will respond and react. If you are offended, you make the choice to respond one way or another. If something makes you angry, before you respond or react, ask yourself why you are offended.

<hr>

I acknowledged what caused me to turn away from my faith and God. I saw it happening with my father, and that's what drove me to realize I couldn't be in this space. I was having self-talk again. I had to accept that it was imperative for me to forgive my father, as well as the people who were around him, connected to him, and condoned his behavior. It became inevitable that I needed a cleansing from all of that because it was starting to become a part of me. The frustration of the church environment, disappointment, and hurt had impacted me to the point that I was carrying out and functioning with my brother the way my father had functioned with us. I'd seen the end result. I'd seen someone hit and hurt in the foyer of the church. Here we were in different situations, years apart, but the optics were precisely the same.

When people watched my father hit my mother, it was abuse. If they were to see my brother and I going at it, they would call it a fight. Why was it okay? No one other than my wife and Mom were trying to pull us apart and be a voice of reason. The spectators and church people were trying to see how it would end. But I couldn't do it. I couldn't devastate my mother the way my father had. When Mom started crying and calling my name, I picked up my ego, anger, and inherited history and walked away gripping my faith. I'd heard that cry before, seen those tears, and it wasn't any different. I refused to allow her to see any more blood. I walked away fuming. I tried to rationalize that since we didn't physically exchange blows, that was progress. It was evident there wasn't any leadership when the objective was to divide and conquer.

Self-talk is a critical concept because it helps you eliminate other voices. If Eve had paused to consider who she was talking to and why, what happened in the Garden would not have occurred. When you give attention that is contradictory to who you are, you need to have a conversation with yourself. Ask yourself, Why am I interested in this? Why did I want to make that decision? Tell yourself the truth. Simple gratification can be destructive. When you start asking and answering these questions, you will place yourself back on the right path—the one God intended.

Engaging in toxicity causes you to separate from who you were called to be. Toxic people feed on negativity and will create it simply to satisfy their need. If you engage in a toxic situation, do it with the objective of ending or healing the situation, not perpetuating what is destructive. Self-talk has kept me from polluting the sacred places of my life. To begin the process:

We need to talk ourselves out of bad decisions. And those bad decisions will occur if we don't ask ourselves why we want to do it.

We must not justify our decisions to do something we know we shouldn't and then label it a mistake. It is not a mistake; it is a choice. People, or society as a whole, should explore why a decision was made.

If your voice is silent, their voices become loud. There is no one in life whose voice should become louder than yours but God.

5.

IT STARTS WITH YOU

"A man's heart deviseth his way: but the Lord directeth his steps."

Proverbs 16:9 (KJV)

~

When God created the world, He did so with humanity in mind, which demonstrated His plan and concern for mankind. The challenge that humanity often faces is trying to align with His plan for our lives. This challenge can lead to choices and behaviors that are often the direct opposite of God's plan. Look at what the challenge did to Eve and Adam. God's plan included and started with them. They were charged to align themselves in obedience to God's plan. God started by making sure the plan was clear and even shared with them the one thing to avoid. God exited the garden so that Adam and Even would be free to decide whether to execute the plan. His exit clearly signified that He had given humanity the free will to decide and carry out His plan for their lives. Notice that God grants unto them freedom. God does not force His creation to do anything; as a matter of fact, He allows His creation to decide. In other words, whatever you are going to accomplish or not accomplish in life starts with you.

Failure or success begins with you. You fail by making the choice not to obey or follow the plan of God. Your spiritual life should take you on a journey that causes you to clearly understand the plan that God has for you. This means constantly using instruments that keep you connected to God. The instruments of studying His Word and prayer are essential to knowing His plan for your life. Can you imagine the longevity of spiritual and physical success Adam and Eve would have had if they would have utilized these two instruments? They had His words that he gave to them. What if they would have trusted and rehearsed what God said and ignored what the serpent was saying? Prayer is the communication between God and man. What would have happened if Adam and Eve had communicated with God after listening to the serpent? They would have both eliminated the distraction and experienced spiritual rejuvenation. This would have led them to stay aligned with God's plan. This is something I have learned to embrace in ministry and life. I lived with a father who utilized the instruments of words and a form of communication disguised as prayer to gain material things such as monetary reward and popularity. Please note I said, "words" and not God's Word. My father utilized the same tool the serpent used to deceive Eve.

This is why it is important to study God's word for yourself so that you are not deceived by what sounds like His word. Because it starts with you, it's important to identify all serpents that are disguised as an asset when they are really a detrimental distraction. The only way to expose the serpent is to see if what is said and done aligns itself with what you know the Word of God has to say. When this takes place, God's plan becomes even clearer, and it is God who will provide you with direction to the place of spiritual success.

Realizing and accepting the fact that I had some of my father's tendencies and behaviors was critical; yet, I needed to stop looking at his history and claiming that I was slowly becoming him. The reality is that what I was becoming needed a self-analysis and then the work to self-correct. If I were to become my father, it would have been my choice.

The anger I had allowed to build came from negative experiences that I didn't give to God. Releasing it—all of it was healthier. It was a process, but I could do it. I was so focused on my father and what he wasn't that I was transitioning into someone I never wanted to become. The only person who could control my feelings and behavior was me. There wasn't any benefit in choosing to be angry. Anger ripped our family to shreds and disconnected us as though that spiritual corruption, drama, pain, hate, rage, dysfunction, and deception belonged in our DNA. But it didn't—we put it there.

I left church that day with the cry of my mother's hurt and

hopelessness digging into my soul. It was painstaking for something that was entirely unnecessary and avoidable. The entire situation caused me to evaluate Lekevie Johnson. No one else. Just me. I could have embraced the fact that I was only reacting because of what transpired with the church and how my brother neglected to speak to our mother. It made sense to have blamed everything on something else and attach culpability to everyone around me. Regardless of how subtle the serpent was, Adam and Eve couldn't blame the serpent. Ultimately, the decision belonged to Adam and Eve just as my decisions belonged solely to me. I walked away from repeating that behavior by challenging it.

I saw the serpent's plan playing out brilliantly. The serpent's whisper was all that was needed to solidify Frentrous's relationship with the Bishop and sever his relationship with Mom and me. The damage was done and still, I trusted God. At the time, the best thing for me to do was remove my focus from them and place it back on God where it should have been all along. People are good at pulling your focus away from what is important to you and placing it on what is important to them. Before you realize it, you will have done exactly what they wanted you to do. You are the one who will allow people to use you if you don't pay attention to how you feel when you are around people that are causing you to change, and not for the better.

The changes I made were immediate because I didn't like how anger made me feel, which was an indication that I had to change. I started on the path of becoming a better man by making a commitment to myself that I would refrain from allowing external pieces to rise up and cause me to become angry. I was so engrossed with my father's history that I hadn't realized I had lost self-control. Doing so opened the door to the realization that others could then control me with and without my knowledge. When I analyzed the choices I'd made, I asked myself: Am I going to permit anger to make spontaneous decisions on my behalf, or am I going to regain control by pausing to deliberate prior to making them? Anger is a choice that causes selfishness and lack of consideration more than anything else. It gives you permission not to care how anyone feels or views you. The objective of anger is to get your point across by any means necessary. Feeling that I didn't have a grip on my emotions was horrible. When I decided to detach from that situation, and the people, I had to determine what I was going to do to maintain my commitment to God. The answer was to consistently work toward it. I had to get back to my relationship with God, praying and engaging in the scripture to be better spiritually. I wanted to possess not only the presence of God in my life but the power and peace of God. I decided that I was no longer the angry kid from Mississippi.

I eliminated the potential of blaming others when I accepted that, it starts with you. Gravitating to the promises of what God has said about me and through His holy writ had to be more important than the opinions and thoughts of anyone else. I needed to have enough discipline to remain clear. I was on the path of cleaning myself up, which was an internal job that started by looking within.

That day, I left church with a heaviness resting in my heart. I went home and spoke with my wife. Rochelle was the person who motivated me because she knew my heart and she believed in me. Rochelle didn't beat up on me because she knew I was already doing that to myself. Instead, she said, "There is so much in you. You have so much potential. You have to go beyond certain feelings." I didn't want to hear her words at that moment because I knew better. I was disappointed that I didn't step away from those destructive feelings; however, that kind of positive support from my wife was important. Rochelle had mastered the art of remaining in a calm space and, in her own way, she makes sure that I meet her there to discuss anything that is disruptive to my spirit or the essence of who I am. After a conversation with my wife, I couldn't change what happened, but I knew one thing I needed to do.

A few minutes later, I went upstairs and tapped lightly on my mother's bedroom door even though it was partially open. Mom was sitting on the edge of her bed, still dressed in her church clothes. She lifted her head and slowly cut her eyes at me in a way that revealed her disappointment. Hugging her first was my non-verbal apology, and then I sat beside her and slipped her supple hand into mine. "Mom," I began, sounding dispirited, "I know this is probably embarrassing for you to see your boys in an unhealthy place. In my effort to protect you, I caused you more pain than anything else. And as your son, it's never my intent to cause you pain. Will you forgive me for stepping outside of what I know is right? Will you forgive me?"

She replied in jest, "No, I will not," followed by soft laughter. Then she said, "I will forgive you. But Kevie, you don't want to ever take anybody through what I've been through or what you've been through. You have to be careful that you're not slowly becoming who you don't want to be."

I lowered my head shamefully and uttered, "Yes, Ma'am."

In my frustration of having tried to do what I thought was right, I asked Mom why she didn't stop me from giving all that money to the church. She explained, "You were so happy and eager to support something that was supposed to be positive and successful. That's who you are, son."

Her words were aligned with what I was feeling. I would not become my father or anyone that God was not pleased with. I held onto my mother's words and kept them at the forefront of my mind, as they had tremendous value and radiated truth. That evening, Mom and I went to dinner where a deeper conversation ensued, creating the perfect opportunity for me to dig into myself. After we returned home that evening, I walked around with a stack of index cards in my back pocket and a pen in my hand. I began to write my path starting with one card at a time. I wrote down what I was going to do with my life, how I was going to fix it, things I wanted to accomplish, and I even described who I wanted to be. I also jotted down on one of the cards that I didn't want to be so angry. Since I learned that nearly anything could trigger me, I was hell-bent on fixing that particular issue. I wanted to be the person who was in control of my thoughts and behaviors. How could I ever lead people if I couldn't manage myself? I wanted to make solid decisions rather than entertain the words of a serpent attempting to make a poor decision appear inviting.

From this point on, it wouldn't matter if I were surrounded by chaos; once I set out to accomplish my goals, that would be my focus. I kept my membership, choosing not to leave that church. I was challenging myself to become a better man of God—practicing and garnering lessons in faith, forgiveness, and patience. Remaining a member of that church was something I had to do at that particular time. I couldn't run as though I'd done something wrong. When we arrived in St. Louis, we were running. Now that I was older, I realized that Mom had reason to leave, as her situation was different; she was running to safety. I needed to stay because I was working on my life. I needed to begin in an uncomfortable place that would demand I practiced discipline and had complete confidence in God. If I left, I would only take the unresolved anger with me. If I truly wanted to become a better man, I couldn't talk about it. I had to walk in forgiveness and faith. Although it was challenging, I knew I was there for a reason. That place of turmoil would become my place of growth. If I were going to grow, the soil had to be rich with what I had to rebuke. We all have those places, and it is up to us to use them to become better individuals.

I was cognizant that I would be sharing space with people who were focused on self-gratification and their own agendas. But this time, I had one, too. My purpose there was not growing professionally—I was seeking a deeper, spiritual growth that would extend into every area of my life. I stayed the course.

When the time came for me to make my departure, a year and eight months had passed; I was ready. I was most pleased that my mother could see, at twenty-six years of age, my relationship with God was paramount. I had matured on a new level and was long past being influenced. I had truly walked in forgiveness—and I felt as though this was the way it should be. I genuinely attempted to love my brother. Although he wasn't able or ready to reciprocate, I was at peace because he had his journey and destiny, which was independent of mine. I could merely pray that time would heal our relationship as well as my brother's relationship with our mother. Shortly after, I left to pastor in Mississippi.

Dad had planted seeds of negativity. As they matured, like dandelions, the wind dispersal caused their seeds to spread. This time, they were sprouting in St. Louis. It was my responsibility to stop the spread of negativity by planting new seeds that would bear healthy and productive fruit to end our generational curse. Back home was a good place to begin.

After everything that happened, there was tremendous value in staying for nearly two years. I remained dedicated to the church because I wanted to find that level of discipline that would keep me serving others regardless of what was going on around me. I served as security, one of the elders, a percussionist, armor-bearer, and sang in the choir. I always wanted to be known as the person who didn't mind serving. The question I asked myself was: Can I undertake serving others when external factors are working against me? Can I stay the course? These were the challenges I faced, and I was drawing on my military career to combat them. I used that discipline to help me succeed in ministry. I knew where I was and what happened, but I served without complaining.

In 2001, I went to Bishop and told him I felt my calling was to head home and start a church. He appeared elated. My wife and I began making plans to move to Mississippi. I wanted to change the entire optics of being in an unhealthy church. However, at that time of my departure, the church was losing its luster and doing poorly. The church was in the middle of a split. Operational issues and power had caused the Bishop and Associate Pastor to reside on opposite ends. I was certain I had already made a solid decision to move on; yet, I didn't know how much so until I heard Bishop tell the Associate Pastor, "Get your people and get the hell out." It was too close to what I was familiar with, and God knew it was my time.

Both the Bishop and pastor had valid points in their intentions to see the church flourish, but there was a disconnect as to how that would happen. The Associate Pastor had been in power and earned tremendous influence in the church. Once it became a church of that magnitude, swelling with people, it was on its way to becoming a notable place in St. Louis. I invested money in the music ministry of the church, which was never repaid. This signified the church still had some work to do in regard to ethics. The Associate Pastor was a good guy, but he and the Bishop couldn't come together, even through mediation. The Bishop simply wanted him gone. I wanted to be the person who separated myself from that negative spotlight and focused on what God had destined for me. It wasn't long before the Associate Pastor found stability and success in his ministry, and I found it was time to follow my destiny. After we left, the church was met with instability—God will remove your relevance.

A part of my change derived from conversations I had with Mom while I was making sure she was okay with the division of her family. You can't undo what is done, but you can move forward and implement changes to improve. Whatever you do in life, don't ever be the cause of your mother's pain. It is something you will not want to see nor will you forget.

The first time I disconnected was because of the things I saw with my father. Admittedly, it took time to realize that disconnecting wasn't the answer. Why would I disconnect, when in all actuality I was keeping myself from arriving at the place God was calling me to be? In my servitude, what I discovered from life was that nothing can get in the way and prevent you from what you have on the inside of you, except you.

I prayed for a resolution to that situation. My prayer was answered. And the question became, What was I going to do now that God had sustained and brought me through that time? I told myself I would never disconnect again. That was the point of starting with myself. I had to find my yes and my no in every situation.

Look at things for what they are, not what you want them to be. Each decision has a beginning, which starts on the inside of us, and as we make them, they teach us to understand ourselves. As soon as something adverse happens, we can pitch a tent and keep building or go back to what is comfortable. Peter the Apostle cut off the ear of the man who went to arrest Christ. However, Christ knew Peter's character. The minute there was adversity, Peter denied Christ not once but three times; after doing so, he gravitated right back to what he knew how to do—fish. Even when our decisions are not in alignment with the will of Christ, He never denies us access to Him. This biblical text was one of mercy and grace. It showed that even after denying Jesus Christ, we could start again. I had seen denial and betrayal, and I had it all inside of me, which let me know I had to start again, but this time, from a different place. Christ started Peter from a place of love.

If it is going to start with you, it can be imperative to reject going back to what you are innately comfortable with. Naturally, growth, progression, and expansion can be uncomfortable. When I was on my journey, there were many uncomfortable things I was exposed to, and if I wanted to grow, I had to overcome these things in the best and most honorable way. When you are serving, there's a potential to be abused by others, and it is important to know when you are in that environment. While you remain connected to your purpose, do not allow that to become a problem. I discovered that as I continued to do the right thing, it appeared to cause discomfort in others.

The ultimate goal was for Mom and I to depart from the church. We felt leadership should display genuine love for humanity and an attempt to bridge or pursue reconciliation rather than separation. The silence spoke greater than anything else. And when people see you, it allows them to see how far off they are. When you keep showing up, it is a reminder of who they are, and they will either want to change their behaviors or push you away. If Bishop and his intimate group could push us away, they would not be reminded of what transpired. Once ill-intentions were exposed, the season changed; the warmth dissipated, and the environment became bitter cold inside the Bishop's intimate circle. Other than that, people treated us well. Despite roadblocks people set in front of you, don't run or avoid them. You don't have to speak or defend yourself; your mere presence can cause others to look at themselves.

The financial guy for the church was the Bishop's brother, and he made his exit within that same year. The things that people were unaware of or chose to ignore had surfaced and become questions. I wanted to leave St. Louis with my faith and plan for my life. God had presented the same opportunity that Eve and Adam had, as well as everyone else. We have the free will to make the choice to serve God, and I made that choice. Consequently, when you arrive at that place, much like the serpent, anyone can approach you with another angle. When you commit to God, don't give in or allow negativity to attach itself to you. Occasionally, there will be disappointments or things that don't go the way you want, and that's okay. Challenges are a part of your growth. If your faith is attached to a person, a place, or a serpent, you will lose your faith when one of them leaves or falls apart.

We cannot blame others for things that occur in our life, as each decision starts with us. Following the Word of God is a choice. Doing what is right or wrong is up to us. If you want to become a better human being, start by looking within, as that is where change must begin.

If you want to change the way you see your life, the way you see others, and remove blame, it starts with you:

1. Start by serving. You will learn so much through your service to others.

2. Take full responsibility, avoid assigning blame, and grow from your lessons.

3. Do not attach your faith to others. I didn't want my faith attached to anyone, not even my mother; if she was hurting, my faith would be impacted.

4. My relationship with God came before my relationship with man, as it started with God.

One thing that I had always been cognizant of is that it wasn't my brother's problem that the church didn't keep its agreement with me. The issue was there were negative seeds planted to make it his problem. Just like Eve and the serpent, chaos was created in a place that wasn't intended to house it. You couldn't find the serpent after it created chaos. It started with Eve, and she wasn't asking questions, or the outcome would have been different. A problem is that we become defensive after the damage is done knowing that we should have said no in the first place. You don't want to be that person, and there is no reason to be; you already know when the answer is a hard no!

I was committed to the path of self-development and self-growth. I learned that it was easy to look at the external factors, but it was more important to evaluate my behaviors and decisions. Many times, I had to ask myself, What about you? When I did, I could see positive changes beginning to happen within myself. I stopped blaming others for any of the bad choices I'd made, my father included. If it doesn't start with you, you will start it somewhere else, and that's where you will make the decision to place blame. When we blame people, it teaches others to do the same and relationships are damaged because of it. Furthermore, it creates anger that can be inappropriately displaced. Once I took ownership, I felt that God was going to take me to the place He wanted me to be. Disconnecting from God wasn't the right decision.

So many times, we attempt to ignore what's obvious and we want to blame others. The serpent was giving instructions that were the opposite of what Adam and Eve were given from God. Why were they taking an interest in what a serpent had to say in the first place?

Standing in the parking lot of a church wanting to fight my brother made it obvious I was angry because I had trusted the wrong individuals. But why? Until I answered that question, it could happen again. When it starts with you, there is an opportunity to turn things around. When Jesus was in His frustration with Peter, He said, "Get thee behind me Satan. You are an offense to Me, for you are not mindful of the things of God, but the things of men" (Matthew 16:23 KJV). Peter had offended God. When he said that, He and Peter were aligned. What did Jesus do in that text? He repositioned Peter. He was no longer aligned with Jesus. Jesus was trying to get to a place, and Peter was trying to stop him from getting there. I had to put the Bishop behind me and follow God.

Sometimes, we have to turn away from a place if it is not in alignment with where we are trying to go. I had accomplished the spiritual growth I was seeking, and the next step was having success in ministry. People will always remember the chaos before they remember what you did to excel. When you are leading people, there is going to be some conflict, and it may not always be the leader's fault; it may be the people.

There comes a time when you have to speak to or rebuke something. I was headed down the path to my destiny. Anything in your life that will disrupt your destiny should be cautionary. I ended the possibility for anyone to derail my relationship with God as this was my priority and I positioned myself to be available for God to use me. There were too many unnecessary and unsavory characters in my life story, which meant I needed to eliminate them. Who extended the invitation? I did! I kept them in my story, although I realized it was time to write them out. Every time I was disconnected from my faith, doing what I wasn't supposed to do, I was giving birth to something undesirable. It was time to cut the umbilical cord because I had been birthing that same attitude and spirit.

The serpent had become a main character of a story that it wasn't intended to be a part of. The serpent was not supposed to take over the story, but its role was to show why it is important for us to say no—and we do possess the ability to say no regardless of how enticing something may be. Saying no is what sustained my desire to pursue what I could never deny; the calling on my life. If anyone should have disconnected from church as a whole, that was the time. I had every excuse why I could have, but the major reason I couldn't is because it was tied to my destiny.

Life presents plenty of excuses, but when you have them in your arsenal, are you going to use them? Again, you have to know when to say no. If you say yes to the excuses, you will be saying no to your destiny. However, once you begin saying no to the excuses, you will be saying yes to your destiny. I decided to say no and put myself in a position to be utilized by God. I couldn't have it both ways; neither can you.

The Bible says, when the Philistines heard that Israel had anointed David king over Israel, his enemies went to attack him. How did David respond to the enemies who wanted to fight him? David found his strength in God. He went down to the cave of Adullam to seek God's direction. David was a qualified fighter, but there was no guarantee of victory. David asked God if he could fight. His assignment was to ask God; after doing so, there was a guarantee. God told David he would be victorious. Sometimes, our actions get ahead of God. We get comfortable in our success and where we are, as well as in our natural abilities. I was not only getting ahead of God, I was ignoring Him.

During that time, we spent the following four months setting up my pastoral installation service to take place in the spring of 2002. It was Bishop who would carry out the Ecclesiastical protocol. We knew a lot of people in St. Louis. It was the place we were engaged and involved in church, and we had built a strong Christian base. It was an exciting time to get off to a healthy start. After my return to Mississippi, during the winter months, Rochelle and I met with Bishop at Barnes Hospital in St. Louis because Rochelle's mother was fighting for her life. Her kidneys were failing from diabetes.

A few months later, we were blessed with the news that Rochelle's mom was well enough to attend my Pastoral Installation Service in Cleveland, Mississippi. Rochelle and I handled personally inviting our Mississippi family and we created a mass mailing exceeding 1,800 invites to people we knew, including one to my father. Rochelle's mom was well connected in St. Louis and loved by many; she personally added numerous invitations. After doing so, Bishop told us to give him all of the addresses and he would send them out and get everything ready for the installation. I had walked in forgiveness and wanted to show him that I had let our history go, so I left it in his hands.

When the event was a few days away, Rochelle's mom was concerned when she spoke with two of her friends who were still waiting on the invitation for the event details but had never received them. Rochelle and I began calling our friends and the responses were consistent; they had never received an invitation. Rochelle's mom was soft-spoken and proper, but she went to Bishop and asked him what happened, as there was no logical explanation. He replied, "The letters and invites must have got lost. The U.S. Postal Service failed us!"

We were told that the church would make all of the calls to follow up and make it an official invite on their behalf as well, yet, no one confirmed receiving that call either. I trusted that time had healed a bitter situation and Bishop would do as he said, but he hadn't changed. We should have handled it on our own. I was hurt. I picked up the phone and made some more calls hoping that I hadn't fallen prey to the serpent again.

August 17, 2002 was a Saturday and the day of my Pastoral Installation Ceremony at Restoration Christian Church in Cleveland, Mississippi. A great deal of preparation had gone into getting to that particular point in my life and preparing for that day. When Rochelle and I arrived, Dad wasn't there. In fact, no one other than Rochelle, Mom, Grannie, my family, Rochelle's family, and Bishop were in attendance. I couldn't fathom how or why that happened. I went through with the ceremony, as it was an honor to become a pastor. Although it may not have looked like it on that particular day, it was my destiny.

The purpose of the installation is an official service that validates that you are qualified for pastoral leadership. Someone must validate that you are ready to serve in this capacity. It is a way of helping a church get off to a healthy start. This turned into Bishop's way of making certain that wasn't the case for me. With Bishop being present at the installation, it made it appear as if he supported my calling and had not contributed to the lack of support. I left his church to begin my own ministry and he was my pastor. I could have asked other pastors to prepare my installation, but since I served at Bishop's church, I did not feel it was appropriate. Besides, the other pastors hadn't seen my work on a regular basis. I worked in ministry with Bishop, so he was the right person to validate my readiness, as he saw the dedication to my work and passion to serve. If he had set aside his disdain for me, he may have been pleased with what I had done and learned.

When I returned home that evening, I began making calls to find out the reason my closest friends and peers had not been in attendance. Over the following few days, I called people to let them know we missed their presence, and people began to respond on their own. Every person I spoke with did one of two things; they either flew into Memphis and drove two and a half hours to Mississippi to visit Restoration and attend at least one Sunday service, or they sent a generous donation for our new church. The support was incredibly humbling because for them, this was about our relationship.

The adversary was attempting to derail my passion by causing me to think I was alone on my journey, thus doubting my destiny. If I was called to do this, I wouldn't be going through all this. Instead, I asked myself what I was going to do from here.

6.

ACKNOWLEDGE YOUR LIMITS

"And he cometh unto the disciples, and findeth them asleep, and saith unto Peter, What, could ye not watch with me one hour?"

Matthew 26:40 (KJV)

~

*T*he reality of life is that you can't control anything but yourself. If you try, you may be the one manipulated or controlled. This is the hallmark of acknowledging your limitations. It's imperative to acknowledge what you can't control so that you can remove your focus from it. This is the lesson that kept me on my spiritual journey to do what God had called me to do. I had to embrace the harsh reality that I couldn't control my father's actions, the lies and deceit, or a bad spiritual leader. What I did was look within to ensure I wouldn't allow the external circumstances happening to become a perpetual part of my life. The only way to free myself was to acknowledge reality.

Limitations are not always negative. They actually provide an avenue for detachment. Let's take another look at the Garden of Eden. Adam and Eve couldn't control the fact *that the serpent existed, neither could they control what the serpent had to say. They were limited in these areas; however, they could control how they responded to the serpent. When you acknowledge your limits, it should drive you to the place of focusing on what you can control.*

The benefit of acknowledging your limits is that it is your personal alarm that sounds when it's time to detach from something or even someone. The issues arise when you ignore the alarm. Eve could have detached herself immediately from the serpent and not entertained it. Eve had total control of telling the serpent no. One "no" from Eve could have potentially silenced the serpent. Instead, the serpent was able to gain control because Eve granted it. Eve became a spokesperson for the serpent and recommended to Adam what the serpent suggested to her. From that point, peace became an absent element in the garden. Adam and Eve had access to the entire garden with the limitation of not eating from the forbidden place. When you acknowledge your limits, you have to remind yourself that life must be lived with certain restrictions. Those restrictions are not bad to have, rather they are a way to keep you focused on your assignment. When Jesus was in the garden of Gethsemane, submitting himself to the assignment of the father, He requested that His inner circle spend some time praying with Him for one hour. To His dissatisfaction, He found them asleep. Jesus did not allow their limitations to keep Him from His assignment. He eventually detached Himself from their inability to stay awake and focused on His divine calling. "Then cometh he to his disciples, and saith unto them, Sleep on now, and take your rest: behold, the hour is at hand, and the Son of man is betrayed into the hands of sinners" (Matthew 25:45 KJV).

W hen my wife and I moved back to Mississippi, I was approaching 26 years of age, and some moments made me feel as though I had never left. Family was everything, and perhaps it's a foundational thing, because I missed my Mississippi family. When I was home, I was able to relax, laugh, and be my jovial, happy self because there weren't any expectations, which was refreshing. Rochelle was being introduced to the dog days of summer—Mississippi in its finest hours and season—mosquito season. That season can't be compared to anywhere else.

Whether in St. Louis, Mississippi, or wherever we moved, Rochelle decided where we were going to live. There was a new subdivision coming up, and she liked the area, so we built our house there. I knew Rochelle was making a sacrifice leaving her mom and family in St. Louis. I knew it wouldn't change the way she felt about being away from her family, but the only thing I could think to do was build her dream home. The problem was that it wasn't in a dream location.

My church, Restoration Christian Church, was just ten miles from Symonds. It was always a childhood dream that I would one day have the opportunity to impact the small community that I came from. It was challenging for us as a new couple, but one thing I was certain of was that my wife was unwavering when it came to my ministry. She did everything she could to push us to a place of success, and we were undoubtedly a team. I loved the way my family embraced her, which was to the highest degree, the same way her family embraced me. That was a critical and attractive piece as to why I returned home. Returning home and having Grannie again was bigger than life.

Leaving St. Louis was bittersweet. It presented a new beginning in a place close to my soul. Two years after we left St. Louis, Rochelle lost her grandmother, Lucille. She was a wonderful woman. My mother had returned home to Mississippi nearly two months before us. She was paving the way for us and doing legwork for the church. The reality is that things had come full circle and brought us back together, without the stress, until we met another tremendous loss. We had gone back to spend time with Rochelle's mom, Flora, every chance we had. My wife struggled each time we left her. I was volunteering at the Boys and Girls Club when her sister, Ralphaelle called to tell me her mother passed prior to telling Rochelle. She was worried about how Rochelle would handle her passing. It was most difficult to take my wife home to St. Louis to be with her sister while they prepared to bury their mother.

Flora passed a few days before our son Kaleb was born. Flora had shown us incredible love. It was awfully difficult because Rochelle, her mother, sister Ralph and grandmother were a close-knit family. To see my wife grieving was heartbreaking.

I began working to lead a ministry in the south with what I had learned. The topic of focus was advancement, and I was coming in with a different approach. I didn't want to have church once a month. My goal was to engage people every Sunday, and indeed it was a challenge. Even though Grannie and Auntie Hattie Bell were committed to their church, they were willing to support mine, too. And seeing them from the pulpit was something special; those were huge life highlight reels. To have my cousins at my church, too—they trusted me with their souls and placed their spirituality in my hands—I couldn't minimize the love, trust, and respect they displayed. I was grateful that they knew me because some people tend to measure a pastor by the commitment level of his family. The involvement, or lack thereof, speaks volumes.

Rochelle and I did things differently. I wanted to eliminate any negative aspects of ministry that humans can induce by alleviating personal conflict with people in the church. I wanted our congregation to have an example of how to function as a body so they could become an example for new members and others in general. Since our family experienced a great deal of pain, I couldn't allow it at Restoration. I saw what it looked like for my mother, the first lady, being ousted by the pastor and congregation. I didn't want to repeat any of that. I was cognizant that our ministry needed to be family-oriented. We were striving to be an excellent example of a pastor and his family. I had begun this process with my wife, who was directly involved. Rochelle knew I wasn't like my father. He was two different people, one masquerading at home and the other in the pulpit. Rochelle and I spoke of protecting our integrity at the highest level and it took work to do that. I was young, but I took on the responsibility to minister the right way. I felt that I had to grow my family spiritually. Our spiritual instruments were studying the Word of God, praying, and having family discussions together. We examined what was being taught at church and in our personal life. Fasting was also a part of our process. Having my family want to attend my church was huge for me; it contributed to my success in ministry.

God said it is not good for man to be alone. The garden was the ministry God assigned to Adam and Eve. They were to preserve what God allowed them to be in charge over, which is what ministry is about—taking care of what God allowed you to lead. Adam and Eve were responsible for growth. God told them to be fruitful, multiply, and increase what he had given them. Ministry is a major responsibility, and it wasn't designed for Adam to try and accomplish the Will of God in ministry by himself. God gave Adam Eve as a support system. "The steps of a good man are ordered by the Lord: and he delighteth in his way. Though he fall, he shall not be utterly cast down: for the Lord upholdeth him with his hand" (Psalms 37:23-24 KJV). If God is ordering my steps and I know the plan He has for my life to prosper and be well, what is the purpose in creating my own path? God and His plan left room for us to make poor choices, but part of the design was that He ordered the steps, which is the course we should take. However, He did not make Adam and Eve take the steps, nor did He with me. As long as what you do and the choices you make do not contradict what His word has to say, it is a yes that you can do it. God is not concerned with some of our most trivial matters, which is why we have free will. We want to treat spirituality as if we are not free, yet we are. God knew there would be a fall that would make us better if we chose to bounce back from it. Our success is by design, but there are going to be some moments when we will have challenges. Surrender to God, He will order your steps and leave room for your mistakes.

Although Adam and Eve were kicked out of the garden, God still covered them with a coat of skin so when they looked at themselves, they would not see their mistakes. An animal had to be sacrificed to do this. The Bible is one complete story, and the covering is an illustration of what is to come on Calvary. God used his physical self to cover our sins. God did not sacrifice an animal; this time, He sacrificed His son. God knew he would have to do more for humanity. Understanding the core principle that there are some things that we are not going to be able to circumvent, we realize we are going to need God in our life. Adam and Eve couldn't get away from that sin. We can forgive ourselves, yet we cannot forgive our own sins—God can. This encourages me to do better, even when my choices aren't good. When God forgives my sins, it gives me a fresh start. We were created with limitations, which is why we need help, support, and encouragement. We must acknowledge our limits.

Restoration was a ministry we started from scratch. We leased a building and started it in a community that was struggling. It is considered the low end of Cleveland, Mississippi: a poverty-stricken area with shotgun houses. The frame houses were older, about 12 feet wide with a door in the front and back. You could see straight through it, and one room was behind the other on one side. If you fired a shotgun through the front door, the bullet would go straight through the house and out the back door, hence the name, shotgun houses.

My ministry and approach were about impacting and empowering people for change. I wanted to change their minds about how they saw life. I didn't want to go to an area where people had money. It didn't mean that because they had money their life was better. I wanted to go where life was hopeless for some—hope was needed to restore faith and work; hard work and consistency could bring change. I thought churches needed to be a great resource center where our doors were open to all. I was young, but I wasn't afraid of what ministry meant. I wanted Restoration to be a hub for the community. It was a red brick building and set on the corner of 1144 S. Chrisman Ave. It had glass, peach-colored doors. A fellowship hall that was a shotgun house was attached to the building. It could seat 100 to 120 people and had four small classroom spaces. That first year was the most difficult, and I could have easily regretted every moment. I didn't want to use or go back to the traditional method in order to win. Some days, I considered having service monthly and then slowly transitioning the church to weekly services. Since I was trying to advance the people, families, and the community, I didn't want to compromise what I thought was a positive initiative, so I stayed the course.

Rochelle, Mom, Grannie, Auntie Hattie Bell, and my cousins came to my 9 a.m. worship. The other churches had an 11:00 a.m. worship, so my family had time to make it to their regular church service, too.

Finances were limited, but I worked as a police officer overnight to have an income to take care of my family and build the church. Working overnight meant I couldn't climb the ranks and get to the dayshift because no one was retiring. Rochelle worked at Delta State University with the Mid-south Delta Tri-Leadership Program. She traveled with her job. We were okay financially and continued to pour our own resources into Restoration. Mom was a licensed daycare provider, so we opened a childcare facility at the church that was licensed by the state. Mom ran it and hired the providers. It didn't take long before the daycare was integrated by families in the community seeking daycare, as we didn't discriminate. Once that happened, it was a gamechanger. Restoration was on the map. We never became integrated as a church, but the daycare did well and provided name recognition. It was the beginning of growth, stabilization, and people knowing who we were. I focused on young people because the church competes with so much else. Youth were my driving point. When I thought of our youth, I thought of longevity. A strong youth component was critical. Parents appreciated their kids being involved in a church with additional parental support. I started a youth conference, which the newspaper covered. We worked to offer something different every year for our youth conference and made it unique. In my three years, we never gave up. We saw steady spiritual growth and established a positive structure with discipline in the way we operated. Our membership had steady growth. We were proud of the job we were doing and could see the progress through the congregation and our reputation in the community we were impacting. We had a service every single Sunday.

In the beginning, establishing our church was challenging, considering we were starting a new ministry that was nontraditional. I would be remiss if I didn't share that some of those days were discouraging, but I was supposed to stay the course—that specific course. I had to acknowledge that I couldn't come in and rush the growth. I needed good people, with honest intentions, who wanted to grow with us. The limitation I had was to trust the process by putting a plan in place and remaining focused and consistent with executing it. I couldn't control the outcome. People often want to control when things happen, but they can't. We are able to manage and trust our process, planning, and execution. I didn't quit when it didn't appear to be happening fast enough. Adam and Eve didn't trust the plan and they stopped executing. They were to name everything, take care of everything, and make sure it was producing. When the serpent came along and tried to get Eve to ignore what she was supposed to do, she should have stayed the course and continued executing.

She couldn't control that the serpent was there and that it was talking, but she didn't have to give it her attention. Adam and Eve were in charge of everything, but listening to the serpent altered their path.

When you become relevant to others, do not turn away from God and attempt the journey your own way. One of the biggest mistakes that the adversary could make with me was to let me get to my Bible and get to preaching and teaching. Let me have the audacity to pray when I am hurting and get words out to say, "God, you see me in my pain,"—this is the beginning of progress, even if it takes time to see it.

Limitations don't devalue us; in fact, they improve us because God has divinely connected us to people who have something we don't. We aren't limited across the board from accomplishing our goals because limitations allow us to rely on our strengths. Eve was supposed to be a support system for Adam, but she devalued her position and entertained the serpent. Sometimes people neglect to see the value in their assignments when they are actually a piece of a bigger picture.

Limitations are about the assignment, not about production. If you get caught up in the productivity and you aren't excited about what you are doing, then you're focused on the restrictions. Assignments aren't designed to limit you, they are designed to produce who you already are. The serpent convinced Eve that God tried to limit her and Adam to everything they had in the garden, as if they didn't have enough. Limitations entice us to wander outside of our assignments. What kind of guardians were they? In Eve's quest for them to have more, they ended up with less.

Limitations that are placed on people have a negative connotation because people believe they are unfairly restricted. That is not the case, because, while God had given Adam and Eve tasks to do, they still had the ability to produce more, which was not a limitation. It was productivity. Eve was enticed to no longer produce, and when you no longer produce, you start consuming. Eve consumed the fruit from the forbidden place.

Everything doesn't fit into where you're trying to go. Of course, you can acknowledge that something is enticing, but recognize when it doesn't fit into the parameters of what you are trying to accomplish. I give authority with parameters because there are limitations within authority.

God never anoints you past your assignment. When you are assigned to do something—that's where your impact is. If you devalue your assignment, you will lose what you were given. You are limited to your productivity. For Eve, there was a desire for more power and independence. When God designs a structure, it is our responsibility to live within the structure He designed for us. There is nothing bigger and greater than a structure designed by God. Eve failed to realize that there was nothing greater than what God had given them. Their effort to find something that did not give them limits changed their course and the course of mankind. It is imperative to live within the structure that has been created for us and value our assignments. What you are trying to do is be competitive in a structure that wasn't designed for competition. When you get outside of that structure, you invite opinions and other adverse things when the limitations should drive you to say no.

When you have a particular assignment, it can take time to master it. Don't look for more when it is not your time to have more. Acknowledge your limits and respect your position; it will help you in other capacities when it is your time. It's okay to want something better, but ask yourself these questions before trying to move outside of your assignment:

1. Is it my assignment?

2. What am I going to do to get it? Am I willing to do anything?

3. Is what I want to do against God's structure that He has built for me?

4. Is it productive? Are the results pleasing to God?

Being mindful of the value of your assignment will keep you on the journey of that particular mission. People are quick to assign a negative connotation to the word "limitations," but they aren't always negative; they keep you within your goal structure. This goes back to discipline.

When you're on a sports team, you can't play all of the positions. If you did, things would not function as they were meant to because you are moving outside of your boundaries.

If you're the quarterback, you are limited to your position. Period. When you are always trying to do something else, you hurt the people around you. We must acknowledge these structures, for, "A double minded man is unstable in all his way" (James 1:8 KJV).

7.

SECURITY IS KEY

"So God created man in his own image, in the image of God created he him; male and female created he them."

Genesis 1:27 (KJV)

~

Staying the course of what you know God has called you to do requires security. Security starts with understanding that God created humanity for a purpose, eliminating self-doubt. To have security, it is imperative to remember and embrace that you are created in the image of God, which teaches us that it is God's desire that humanity becomes like Him. Considering His desire for us, it is important to purge anything or anyone that will encourage taking a path in life that distracts us from being more like Him. This is another lesson that I had to learn.

With everything that had taken place in my life, I had to realize it was designed to keep me from becoming more like Christ. A shift in what I was looking at was important in submitting to God's plan for my life. The most important element to focus on was the fact that God cared so much about us that He created us with Himself in mind. This provides not only security but the confidence to stay the course. I had moments in adverse life experiences that caused me to be insecure. I struggled to trust people, and I was not confident that my faith was necessary. This was largely due to the fact that I hadn't spent enough time looking within. I spent my time looking at others when I should have been looking to God. There is always a reason or excuse as to why we make the choices we do. I had attached God to the awful actions of people—including my father. If we can only see God through the poor behaviors of others, then it will consistently derail us from our place of faith and relationship with God.

Security is rooted in knowing who we are in God and maintaining a relationship with Him. When the relationship is not maintained, it leads to choices and decisions that contradict the image of God. The maintenance of the relationship requires some simple yet important practices. Prayer and consistent study of the Word of God are two important practices that are critical to maintaining a healthy relationship with God. When the relationship is healthy, it builds security. When security is present, it grants the confidence to say no to things and the very people who will show up specifically to derail your assignment. Adam and Eve could have told the serpent no if they had been secure in their relationship with God.

In my early years, I struggled to find myself. The conclusion was that I'd wasted years fighting my destiny. I wasn't learning from my experiences, surroundings, or the people around me. I simply wasn't a good student. In time, a thorough reflection caused me to realize that my father wasn't a good student, and he was one of my teachers. He wasn't learning what he needed to, and perhaps he hadn't followed the best examples. I don't know precisely what caused my father to take his path, but, for some reason, he wouldn't depart from it, and in the end that's between my father and God. For many years, I believed a contributing factor to his unwillingness to change was the people in his network giving him one pass after another to be whoever he wanted without consequences. Dad was physically abusive. Clearly, he became comfortable enough to hit my mother whenever and wherever it suited him. When he struck Mom at church, it should have been an automatic dismissal as the pastor of his church, and every other church he pastored. Instead, heads turned the other way; entertainment was an attraction. Dad gave it to them, as he loved that aspect more than honoring the Word of God. What I heard when they responded to my father's preaching was nothing more than noise. They didn't really look at the man they were applauding. Would you watch a man abuse a woman and cheer him on? There is nothing acceptable about that. It should have been infuriating, and the fact that it wasn't scared me, even as a child. Why do we tolerate negative behaviors? Why are there double standards? Why did no one stand up to stop it? Look within and ask yourself these questions.

My father's network allowed him to get close enough to witness and learn the weaknesses, struggles, and sins of those in it. And just as he knew theirs, they knew his—though not all of them, because they didn't see what happened within the walls of our house. Dad's network had collected a plethora of derogatory information on one another, allowing them to maintain longevity with their relationships and positions. How could they condemn my father's behavior when theirs was questionable or condemnable? These secrets and negative behaviors created a sense of security in the lives of so many. It seemed that my father had more dirt on them than they had on him, because no one took him on. It appeared as though Lloyde Johnson was untouchable. If there was a standard for leadership and the pastor wasn't meeting the standards, how could they judge one another or cast the first stone? The politics of it all was how the early regime stayed in power. They led without knowing one another's potential. Their focus was on where they struggled. If they ever wanted to rise up against something my father did, they couldn't. I knew this because, over the years, I had witnessed many of their behaviors. I knew the fundamental difference between right and wrong, and their behaviors were a clear indication that something was not right.

People attach themselves to what moves them— sports, music, business, politics, hobbies, and anything else. Dad had a high level of external respect because of his natural talent, and he used it to move people. He had so much swag in singing, playing instruments, and exciting people that it became his reputation. Whenever I returned home to Mississippi, I often heard some sort of comparative analysis between my father and me. It doesn't settle well with me and I try to separate myself from that because I am Lekevie Johnson, not Lloyde. I had to learn that his history was not my history, and his path was not mine, either. You cannot allow the negativity of others to be attached to your fabric or it will pull you in the direction it is heading.

Home felt good. For some reason, one of Dad's best friends, Andrew Williams, who knew many of his black holes, helped me navigate away from the people who would be detrimental rather than beneficial to me. In 2004, Andrew gave me the opportunity to preach at his church. Most of Andrew's congregation knew my dad. Unfortunately, they'd turned a blind eye to Dad's reputation. It was imperative to show them who I was; a man practicing what he was preaching. I had work to do in proving it. Andrew had appeared to be a close friend of my father's when I was a child. However, by the time I returned, they had disconnected. Andrew had changed the course and moved away from derogatory behaviors and reputations. In my eyes, Andrew was trying to rewrite his legacy; one can be considered guilty, even by association, so it was good to see. I think Andrew wanted to change some of those dynamics and he began immediately. He became overly protective of me, and I continued learning from him. In the forthcoming years, we became very close.

Andrew told me, "If people don't see you, they will hear you. Now you definitely have some of your dad's talents and gifts, but you have your own way of sharing your message with intellect." I knew he was right. People would gravitate to me because of the way my father pastored and that should have been an honor. Conversely, my thought process was that whatever Dad had, I didn't want. I didn't have any desire to have a gravitational pull on people for the wrong reasons. I was not willing to entertain a congregation in the pulpit for financial gains, laughter, cheers, or noise. I grew up and lived without the security of my father, Lloyde Johnson, but I would not resign to live with the absence of God, as He is my security.

I couldn't understand how people close to you or that you are supposed to lead spiritually can ignore such demeaning, derogatory behavior. I heard my father preaching "God is love," but I saw him displaying hate. God is peace, but my dad disturbed the peace. What caused him to live this way?

My return to Mississippi taught me that most of Dad's people were trying to turn the corner, but he hadn't. One day, Mom was in town and we ran into Dad at a funeral. I heard my mother say, "Lloyde, you were sick. But I had to forgive you on my own." I never heard him apologize to Mom, but her forgiveness was instrumental in changing me.

If we cannot change ourselves, how effective can we be in changing others? How is it that we can identify the flaws in others so clearly, but not our own? How could I come home and live in that town and not have forgiven him? You cannot build relationships with everyone, but you should not set out to destroy them. I was able to survive what I'd been through with Bishop because I walked in forgiveness and demonstrated it while I was still there. I had to practice everything that I would preach or want from others. It didn't make sense how others found security in what my father had to say and sing about but didn't know and overlooked how he lived. I always wondered why my father wasn't held accountable for his behavior. In time, after my own attempts to do so, I came to understand that some may have tried.

I made the decision to return to Mississippi because I had grown secure in my relationship with God; I could not go home, had I not. I knew that I would face serpents throughout my journey, but I simply could not listen to them or entertain their ways. Nonetheless, I wanted my father to hear me.

I believed that for me to be successful in ministry, I had to be able to love a guy who didn't love us back. Sometimes, I helped or ministered to people who didn't love me, God, or even themselves. But it was my responsibility to teach them and show them what love was about.

I was elated to be asked to preach a service in Rosedale, Mississippi by Pastor Littleton. Unfortunately, she was not entirely accepted in the religious community. Her service was in a storefront. She was really close to my dad. I preached for her unbeknownst that my father was going to show up that night. After my sermon, she said to the congregation, "Wouldn't it be nice if we could get Big Johnson and Little Johnson to sing a song together?" I normally would sing, but that night, I hadn't gone into a song. Dad made his way from the last row, nodded to me, and said, "I don't know what my boy may know. Maybe I can do something familiar for both of us. 'Build me a cabin in glory,'" he suggested, and we sang together like we'd been singing together my entire life.

That night, Dad and I talked a little more. He asked how church was going. I told him it was good. He followed up with, "Isn't it time that you start singing with your daddy?" My initial thought was no. Since I didn't respond, he looked me directly in my eyes and repeated it.

"I'll get back to you on that," was all I could say. I had never contemplated singing with my father before then. How could I? Our relationship was practically non-existent. But I went home and thought about it because I wondered if I would have the opportunity to impact my father. If he was around me enough to see who I was and what God was doing in my life, would it inspire him? Could I walk in forgiveness along this entire journey? I considered it to be an opportunity to heal both of us on a deeper level.

My mother walks in forgiveness. When she forgives— she truly forgives. She has supported me along my journey and never wavered. I trust my mother explicitly, which is the reason I rely on her for guidance. When I spoke to my mother about my father's offer, she didn't tell me not to go near him. Her primary concern was for me. She wanted me to pay attention to what I was seeing so that I would not become it. Mom already knew everything I would be facing. Her sole objective was that I would not be enticed or influenced. After everything my father did to her, it was humbling that she supported giving our relationship the chance to heal.

Before determining that I would sing with my father's quartet, Rochelle and I had a discussion, as she was well aware of the history. Both Rochelle and Mom understood what it was I was attempting to do. I had to practice what I was preaching; forgiveness and accountability were a part of it. I wanted to hold my father accountable and, at the same time, I held myself accountable. I wanted him to see me and know that God was using me, not him.

Mom and Rochelle were close, and they had in-depth conversations about me being out on the road. Mom cautioned me to be careful of that environment and remember to remain respectful of my wife; that would never be a factor. Rochelle agreed to accompany me whenever possible. When she didn't, we would talk after every single engagement. I spoke with Mom regularly, too. It made me think of the dinners we had as a kid with Grannie; that was our reality check.

I had been with Dad for 3 to 4 months. He didn't hide how he was, and if I didn't say something to him, it would have been as though I was saying I was okay with it. I should have been able to say what I witnessed was shocking or surprising, but somehow it wasn't. I wondered if Dad ever asked God if he could have a fresh start. Then I questioned if he ever had a relationship with God, because it didn't seem as though he had any degree of consideration for other people. How do you profess to be a believer of Christ and not be considerate of others? Adam and Eve, the only two people on earth to birth all of mankind, had no reason to be selfish, yet self-gratification was more important than anything else. They must not have considered everything they were connected to.

I believed my father didn't want me to have success. He wanted me to have ugly flaws attached to my reputation so that he could have no accountability and not feel judged by his son. When we traveled together, there were things I brought to the atmosphere in the van that irritated Dad. He was a blues lover to his core. As we went from Mississippi to Arkansas, I'd say, "Pop, we can't listen to gospel music? We're getting ready to go minister to some people after listening to blues. I'm not going to be the entertainer— you are—and there is no God in your behavior, but we are singing about God?" I was a thorn in his flesh when it came to being connected to him. I presented a level of spirituality that he never considered or wanted. When I spoke about spirituality, he became visibly uncomfortable. Dad would turn away from me or spew a few curse words to cause the other group members to laugh, cleverly dismissing what was said. The majority of the time, when Rochelle came to the service or to see us perform, we drove together rather than ride with the group.

Early one morning, all nine group members, including Dad and me, were on our way to Monroe, Louisiana to perform for a Sunday service. We were in our old sandy-grey, 15-passenger van with a blue trailer in tow carrying our instruments and everything we needed for the show. We were an hour or so into that four or five-hour trip including time for a breakfast stop. I was trying to get the van to quiet down so I could engage them in spiritual conversation. Dad sure could preach—but he wasn't willing to talk about anything that was good or healthy. He was quick to circumvent those positive conversations. I don't think he wanted to put himself in a situation where he could be challenged in regard to the scripture, either. He was shrewd when it came to getting everyone else to laugh so he could control the conversation. Anything that led to dialogue about real religion, God, our goals, or life was quickly dismissed.

That morning, as soon as I began to speak, Dad shouted, "Look at my boy, Mr. Holy Roller." He had become critical of me so the group would ignore my spiritual conversations, questions, or anything he deemed would make him look bad. "Look at my son! Look at him go," he laughed and turned away to begin another conversation about the groupies. Of course, there were occasions when his group of guys laughed with him because he was jovial. On other occasions, they were laughing at him. I didn't think Dad could distinguish between the two types of laughter and, if he could, it didn't seem to matter.

Dad got away with being that version of Lloyde Johnson. No one in the van would say anything to him, as Dad had authority over his group. If they were eating from the table of Pharaoh, who supplied everything, they couldn't tell Pharaoh how to act. Dad bought the Columbia blue and white uniforms, paid for the meals, and picked everyone up to travel with him. He knew how and what to do for the group, and he was all in. It was an indication that he knew how he should have taken care of his own family but didn't.

With nine grown men in the van, the temperature was already becoming uncomfortable. The stench of Kool and Newport cigarettes made it difficult to breathe, especially since I didn't smoke. I unclamped my window, pushed it open, and turned my head toward it as though I was trying to survive by syphoning air from outside. Dad was in his normal derogatory, nasty demeanor. His conversation was merely locker room talk about his quartet groupies who traveled miles to hear us sing. He was pleased with himself, boasting about the things he did. "They were just groupies," he said, as if they didn't matter. He was married again, but his behaviors hadn't changed.

I turned and said, "Wow. That's how Mom had to live? With that? This is what you were doing when you were with my mom?"

Dad slammed his hand on the shoulder of the passenger side of his seat and flippantly exclaimed, "I'll tell you what, Lekevie Johnson, don't do anything you see me do!"

I glowered at him, concluding, he knew right from wrong.

But if he knew better, why didn't he do better?

Perhaps he decided that he'd reached the climax of his life and there was no need to improve upon his behaviors because he wasn't trying to go any further or make anything better. He knew who he was and how he had lived. There were moments when Dad seemed as though he was in the final stage and go at his life. When you feel there is nothing else to be done, there is no motivation to make any adjustments.

I don't think the afterlife was ever a concern with Dad because he was a people-pleaser and not a pleaser of Christ. Those are two conflicting personalities and lifestyle types with different conclusions.

It became apparent that my father, the same man I'd always known, was not going to stop or change who he was. The issue I had was that he told me not to do what he did rather than attempt to become an example of the kind of man I should want to be. I said, "Dad, you don't want me to do anything you do?" He shook his head, but it wasn't out of shame, because he boldly continued on his path. Challenging the integrity of what he was doing brought a level of accountability that it didn't appear he ever had or expected to face. Accountability is necessary, just as Adam and Eve were held accountable.

When we arrived at the service, Dad normally would come out and sing "Walking With Jesus Every Day Of My Life," but after I returned to Mississippi and began singing with his quartet, Dad and I wrote a song that we sang together, "Lord If You Move, I'll Fall." He would begin the selection by reciting, "I am getting up in age now, and it's good to have my son with me. Old men are for wisdom and young men are for war." Then he would gloriously sing a couple of verses nice and slow and turn it over to me. But that particular night, after our exchange in the van, he was upset with me. Dad didn't give that spiel, and he didn't let me sing as much as he typically did.

I could deal with that because, after nearly ten years of not having my father in my life, I had a lot to say. Seeing that he hadn't changed gave me even more of a reason to speak up. I didn't have a lot of words because I was never one to disrespect my father. If I had told him all of the things I had held inside for years, we likely wouldn't have reconciled. I didn't return to Mississippi to one day leave without understanding, healing, and forgiveness. I didn't go there to create a greater division between us, either. I said what needed to be said and let him reflect on my question.

I could have left the group and decided I wasn't going to deal with any of that, but I stayed because it made my father realize that I was holding him accountable. And he knew that. Dad could have kicked me out of his group, but he didn't. As long as I was around, I was a thorn in his flesh. I enjoyed seeing Dad uncomfortable because it meant he heard me. I wasn't being vengeful; it allowed me to see a different side of him—a side that knew better. I was holding my father accountable because I was learning to love my father, and I think he was trying to love me the only way he knew how.

We traveled all over Louisiana, Mississippi, Arkansas,

Alabama, and Chicago playing in front of packed houses. Back then, 200 to 300 people was a nice church crowd. We even did festivals. Pastor Lloyde Johnson and New Tradition was the headliner for Morgan Freeman's Gospel and Blues Festival. Before I joined the group, it was called the Sensational Voices of Hope. Dad recorded an album called Call on Jesus.

I listened to and trusted God, which was everything. I'd specifically quote scriptures to cause Dad to reflect on his opposing and manipulative behaviors. It seemed as though he was internally fighting God because he wasn't secure in his relationship with Him.

I asked my father what made him physically abuse my mother because I wanted him to know I remembered who he really was. His response was non-verbal—four wrinkles formed in the center of his forehead. I knew who he was and what he was. Once he knew that vision was still at the forefront of my mind, it made him uncomfortable, although he never responded. There were boundaries that I would not push and things I could not change, but my presence would remind him that he, too, could be better. There was still hope if he was willing to do the work.

Over time, as my relationship with God, my family, and ministry evolved, my anger and hurt over the abuse, abandonment, and neglect diminished. I still had this accountability piece and moments when I continued to ask questions so they wouldn't stay buried inside of me. When I looked within, I didn't want anything that wasn't good inside of me. I asked why he never came to St. Louis but, as expected, he changed the subject; he didn't have an acceptable or valid answer. He wasn't willing to look within to give an honest response, and he knew that I wouldn't accept anything other than the truth.

I should have struck up more conversations when no one else was around, but the reality was that he rarely allowed one-on-one time. Dad would not engage in serious conversations that would cause him to evaluate his life, and after being around him, I believe it was because it could have had a serious impact on him. There was no way Dad could look at me without thinking about what he did to his family. Perhaps asking me to join his choir was his way of trying to reconcile the past the only way he could. There was another influence that was never spoken of that kept Dad from changing. Change is a process, and he wasn't willing to take that on.

Initially, I couldn't wrap my mind around Dad's ability to write so many songs that caused people to step away from sin and seek a deeper relationship with God—yet, it didn't change him. After being around my father more, I came to find that he stayed away from serious and relevant conversations about God. I don't believe he invested time in continually studying the Word of God and learning the proper context of the scriptures. His preaching was surface level, but his voice went below the surface—it was strong, prominent, and persuasive. That alone kept him relevant.

Being around my father wasn't about him, it was about me.

When I was younger, I wanted to seek vengeance for what he'd done to Mom, but that anger, rage, and hurt turned into forgiveness. That was the best thing that could have happened. I needed to learn from Dad. His history, the other pastors, deacons, and people around him had tremendous value. I took in what was beneficial without becoming distracted by any of the negative behaviors. Distractions pull you in the wrong direction when your attention is needed elsewhere. I was there because I wanted to see where and how things went wrong and why there was no security in God.

Mississippi was good for me. I had Grannie, my family, my ministry—Rochelle and I were happy. I was so different and aligned with God that I couldn't be shaken or removed from what I knew was right. I was secure in my role, and I believe others could sense it when they saw me. I felt a wave of support from other pastors. Andrew continued to be a huge mentor and supporter; Tom Meeks was another, as well as Pastor Scurlark, who pastored less than a mile from Dad's church. Scurlark and I grew up together; Dad was his pastor. Given my route was a bit different, Scurlark was in ministry before I was. Then there was Pastor Strotter. His father and Dad sang together. Strotter was another one of the guys who embraced my ministry and returned home. He brought positivity and support. There were other pastors who knew my father and his reputation, but these particular gentlemen gravitated to me upon arrival. They were trying to be supportive and offered their assistance to keep me on the right path. I had no intention of veering off, as I had done that in the Marines, seen what happened to my father, and, for some reason, the history and decisions of Adam and Eve stayed with me.

Like Andrew Williams, Pastor Tom Meeks was instrumental in bringing me to his church. He allowed me to preach and gain exposure, since I was building a ministry from scratch.

I wanted to build a ministry that lifted and encouraged people through teaching. When people learn, they have the choice to apply those lessons. Andrew and Tom had churches in Rosedale, Mississippi, which was a stone's throw from Symonds. Andrew and Tom weren't threatened by my personal gifts, primarily because they weren't insecure with their own. Since I was Lloyde's boy, they treated me as though they had to help me. Although they were generous with opening their churches to me, I didn't preach at Dad's church, Sykes Chapel, until I had been home for six years. Dad offered me an invitation, not because he thought I was ready but because his pastor, who preached at my father's church for his Pastor of Celebration anniversary every year, was involved in a scandal. Dad was trying to detach himself from that situation, so he asked me to preach as the backup, and I came off the bench. I was pleased to let his congregation see how different Dad and I actually were. I wanted them to see the growth I'd had while living in St. Louis, being raised by Mom, and then being in the Marines. I wanted his congregation to realize that Lloyde Johnson didn't raise me and then see the outcome. I wanted Dad to bear witness to who I was, too. You can feel truth, hear integrity, and the spirit of God is undeniable. Undeniable. My father had only visited my church, Restoration, one time when I came home. I had an annual Pastoral Celebration, too, but Dad never came to that.

Andrew Williams invited me to his church on a regular schedule. I preached a series of services, three nights a year, for his revival. I was amazed by the way he embraced me and the way I was received by his congregation. I wasn't sure what to expect from people and felt they would stay on the sidelines and let me pass or fail because I wasn't like my father, and it seemed as though we were cast away. I didn't know what people knew, thought they knew, or how they felt, but I worked hard and was consistent with being secure in my relationship with God. It didn't take long before the people in our community became aware of the fact that I was trying to write a different path. I was trying to pull from what is right, beneficial, and good to utilize other resources instead of relying on what I thought I knew. I needed their experiences and their wisdom.

Often, people are guilty by association. People are curious in nature, and some will dissect what pastors and their associates have in common. At one point, I questioned Andrew's motives. I was cautious because I wondered if he was going to affect my reputation. Andrew had two established churches and was successful in real estate. However, public opinion can hold people accountable for their reputation and stifle their growth. Accountability is a good thing, though, to my knowledge, Andrew never held Dad accountable. Dad was still standing the same way he always had. But for some reason, Andrew held me accountable to my values, destiny, and commitment to God.

If there was a whisper of negativity with my return home, it never met my ears. Had there been any, I expected that it would have come from Dad because he didn't seem happy that I had returned or proud that I had become a pastor. Perhaps it was that he didn't want me to become him. But I stayed and I was immune to having the type of lifestyle that he chose. I was living my life in alignment with Christian principles and morals—the direct opposite of what Dad was doing.

At that time, there weren't many places to go in Mississippi, but Rochelle and I did a lot of things together even if it was just going to the post office. "Johnson is afraid to leave home without his wife," others joked. The truth was that I loved doing as much as I possibly could with my wife. Rochelle and I didn't plan it that way, it was organic for us. Nevertheless, when people noticed, it meant they were watching. Mom said it was a compliment. I agreed and continued to embrace it as such.

I took in what I could of my father's ministry's composition when he was married to Mom. I knew the people that were still there remembered, too. At Restoration, I wanted to draw couples and families to our ministry, along with individuals who wanted to know God, improve their lives, and grow to become better. My goal was to cultivate a wholesome environment rather than an entertaining show or playground for adults. I worked to set a positive example and be supportive of the entire congregation, and I knew it would be a challenge to draw people into this type of environment. The best way to do it was to be a good example for them. People needed proof and a track record that made them more comfortable. I needed to show them that good example every time they saw me, and I could only do that if I was living that way. I am human just like them, but I had established the goal of continually striving to be better in the eyes of God. Better people make churches, communities, and the world better. If Adam and Eve had invested their time in getting better and taking care of the garden rather than being distracted by the serpent, imagine how things could have been. What would happen if we spent that energy focusing on being our best?

I had spent a lot of time angry with my father, but I forgave him. I didn't know why he did the things he did, but that was his conversation to have with God. I was his son and not his jury, so I had to live that way. He was a pastor, but, like Adam, Eve, and me, he was human. Forgiving my father was a part of becoming a better man. As long as I was growing spiritually, I knew I could make those around me better, which is one of the reasons I worked on myself every day.

It took five to six years before people from Symonds and the surrounding communities began making their presence known at Restoration. I found through conversations with them that they'd come because of name recognition, and they wanted to see how long I was going to be there. I didn't have a Baptist title associated with my church, as it was non-denominational. At that time, Baptist churches were dominant in Mississippi. Some of his members would come by my service and still make their 11 a.m. service. Most came to hear Lloyde Johnson's boy, not Lekevie Johnson, only it wasn't that type of service.

I learned that, for some, it wasn't about change, but they heard me. One thing my father and I had in common was singing, and Dad could sing. I think some of them wanted to see how much like my father I was, but I felt I disappointed them. I could definitely sing—but ministering was my focus, and it came through even in song.

Preparation was a priority. I started preparing for the community in which we were establishing our church from the onset, which is why I named the church Restoration, a name which implies value. I wanted to remove the entire mindset and negative perception of church being present but not impactful. I wanted Restoration to be what the Word of God intended the church to be.

When I preached, I planned nearly three years ahead with my messages. The thing about that was my father would call me early on Sunday mornings and ask, "What are you preaching about?" Then he would prepare the same sermon for his congregation. Dad didn't hide it, he told me that he was preaching what I selected. People that attended his church told me, as though I had taken my father's message. It never bothered me because at least he was giving out good information. The difference between what my father preached and what I prepared is that my sermons started with Lekevie Johnson. God provides messages that apply to both the giver and receiver. I needed them. They helped keep me connected to and focused on God.

One of the things that prepared me for what I wanted to present was that I'd had on-the-job training from a young age. I'd been attending church long enough to learn what I should never do. In St. Louis, Bishop had a Pastor School of Ministry, which was a quality program. Carlton Pearson was one of the people who was mentoring Bishop on developing the school of ministry. He was the pastor of the Higher Dimension Evangelistic Center, which was one of the largest churches in Tulsa, Oklahoma with an attendance of over 6,000 in the 1990s. Carlton developed the AZUSA, which was the stage to be on. They recorded live at AZUSA and he was the host of their conference. It was the African-American Pentecostal-Charismatic Movement, which was the style of worship during that time. Carlton went to the Oral Roberts Institute and was mentored by Oral Roberts. He was one of two African-American ministers that hosted a weekly television show, reaching hundreds of thousands. The pastor had high-profile individuals involved with his program, and his church was on its way to becoming quite sizable. The theological information, conversations about the Bible, understanding historical context, overall engagement, and word study was excellent. Bishop was thorough in how he presented scripture, and I was drawn to that. He provided the substance; however, in time, I saw another layer and then another. His lack of application reminded me of my father.

In time, Carlton Pearson's platform went to shambles. When you have that knowledge and understand it but twist it, your life will become twisted, too. Bishop Walter Hawkins was a part of that circle, and when things began to change, it appeared that he pulled away from Bishop. When you are rooted in God in the right place that is aligned with the Word of God, there will be no reason to uproot and leave. As I was learning the Biblical principles, I was applying them. I needed this but not everything else. I was gleaning from their expertise and mindset. I needed their resources, as they were critical. Adam and Eve did not utilize their resources, which was God. This allowed me to reach a place of success and become secure in what I wanted to do. I took that which was beneficial and discarded everything that contradicted where I was trying to go. Being secure in your vision and the purpose God has for your life helps you stay on the path and ignore anything that contradicts that path. If you are not secure in what God is doing and lack a foundational base, you are more likely to be negatively influenced, which happened to Adam and Eve.

Pastor Larry Williams, who is Pastor Strotter's father, is my Godfather. He took Mom to the hospital when I was born. He combined two churches to make one big church and started having church service every Sunday. Some churches were resistant to that because they didn't want to lose their singular identity. Larry Williams went all four Sundays, and since I was used to it in St. Louis, I just flat-out did Sundays from the time we opened. People told me to start with one

Sunday and build from there, but when they thought about it, they realized that having church every Sunday made sense. The mileage with traveling and going from one city to another didn't make sense when there was another option. There are always options. Churchgoers had problems with logistics at first, which was the reason some churches had Sunday service once a month. However, in some churches, people attend Sunday school.

My aspirations were to present a picture that was beyond me. It helped me in ministry. It was the piece that Dad and some of his people were missing. The more you present yourself, the more you miss the spirituality of God. It becomes self-consuming. People can't see God because they are busy making sure they see you. The people in Dad's congregation enjoyed him, and that's why they overlooked the things that happened. The truth behind enjoying Dad was that there was little, if any, change or progress. When you enjoy God, he changes you. When you enjoy people, they entertain you. When you have a relationship with God, if you truly have it, it's for the purpose of change.

The garden became more about Eve. If it had been about God, who had given them everything, there would have been no way a serpent could have influenced them to disobey God. You should never gravitate to negative influences. The serpents and negative external factors exist today, but what you know on the inside of you has to have more influence on your actions. When you are secure in your relationship with God, it drives you to stay the course and make the right decisions about what God is calling you to do. You will have passion, purpose, and focus, and know your destiny. When all of the external vices gain your attention, doubt filters in, and when you truly have a relationship with God, doubt should never be an issue.

When I accepted the call of God on my life, it was about Lekevie Johnson. What I was taught when I left the country started to dwindle. When you know better, you have to force yourself to do the opposite of what you know is right, which takes more mental energy. You can become exhausted just trying to go in the wrong direction. I spent more energy trying to make sure I wasn't doing what I was supposed to do, and it was draining. All of it. The challenges I continuously encountered caused me to take an internal look. Eve listened to the serpent, and then recommended what it said to Adam. They didn't look within or say no.

Security is key. Regardless of what is taking place around you or to you, be secure in your relationship with God.

1. You must be willing to learn how to be secure.

2. You have to believe in God's plan for your life.

3. You have to practice and execute the
   plan to maintain security.

4. Utilize resources that are aligned with that execution.

5. Take time to study the Word of God.

8.

GREATNESS HAS A RESIDENCE

"I can do all things through Christ which strengtheneth me."

Philippians 4:13 (KJV)

~

When God created humanity, He equipped them with every tool they needed to discover greatness. Those tools were connected to their spirituality. This has become the missing element as individuals attempt to reach their full potential. The greatest tool that God has given to humanity is intellect. It is from that intellectual place where one discovers greatness has residence on the inside of them. However, intellect can be misused. When there is a risk of accepting mediocracy, complacency ensues. These are both characteristics that diametrically oppose the characteristics of greatness. When mediocracy and complacency attach themselves to your intellect, there needs to be an immediate mental shift.

This shift must be a spiritual one. Shifting and remaining in a spiritual place will lead to not only acknowledging greatness on the inside of you but also being propelled to walk in that greatness. Greatness is a lifetime spiritual journey that is demonstrated through your relationship with God. When you follow His plan for your life, it propels you to the place of having an impact on the lives of others. One of the worst things that humanity can do is encourage one another to make decisions outside of God's plans.

When His plan is ignored or not followed, the greatness inside of you lies dormant. When this happens, your life becomes like a stagnant tree in the winter, shedding leaves. Remember, when you are operating in greatness, the seasons do not matter because greatness reigns in all seasons. This is because of the spiritual growth characteristic that's involved with greatness. This growth can only take place when there is a consistent connection to a great God. When humanity stays connected to God, He alone gives them the inner strength to face and overcome any demand that life presents.

This is the conclusion that Paul reaches in Philippians 4:13: "I can do all things through Christ which strengtheneth me." That the God that's within me grants unto me the power to face all the external things that life presents. Looking within to the God on the inside of you is where your greatness is. The serpent didn't force Eve to eat from the forbidden place; likewise, Eve didn't force Adam to eat from the forbidden place. It was spiritual dormancy. Spiritual dormancy is the lack of faith that keeps humanity from following God's plan. When your Faith is activated, your greatness is alive. Conversely, when your faith is not activated, failure lurks.

was creating a mental picture of the perfection and greatness that was in the garden. I thought about how God created humanity and connected them directly to the greatness that He created. He placed humanity right in the midst of what was flawless. He gave Adam and Eve the manpower, intellect, and everything needed to take care of what He had given them. When they stopped paying attention to the greatness in the garden, they did not tap into the greatness inside of them.

When we stay connected to and aware of God's presence, it allows us to overcome negative external factors. As appealing as they may seem, those things don't make you great, but they can initiate chaos. We are great because God is on the inside of us. "Ye are of God, little children, and have overcome them: because greater is he that is in you, than he that is in the world" (1 John 4:4 KJV).

The minute I disconnected from God was when I began asserting my own authority and detached from my greatness. Such as Adam and Eve, it was reduced. If you want to understand what changed in your life, or what's wrong, ask yourself why you disconnected in the first place. I knew I'd stepped away from my relationship with God as soon as I decided to appeal to what I wanted—my naughty nature— the flesh. When you disconnect from Him, you disconnect from the greatness on the inside of you. A life absent of God is a life that is open to everything. Eve was open to the serpent, as there was no longer consideration to what God commanded or was allowing them to experience.

Every time I felt that I had made a poor decision, I already knew why. I was well aware of the choices I should have made because I knew right from wrong, just as you do. You can feel it, too. You have to make a decision to ignore that tug on your conscience when it's warning you something's not a good decision.

One experience after another served as a lesson and reminder that it was not possible for me to live apart from God. In order to rebound, it was necessary to redirect my attention to the Word of God. Adam and Eve should have asked themselves why they were allowed to be blindsided by mediocrity. They had everything in the garden but transitioned to a mediocre mindset that focused on one tree and one forbidden fruit when they already had so much to enjoy. There was nothing they needed to say except "no" to the serpent. There was nothing I need to say other than "no." In entertaining the option to appeal to the flesh, I opened myself up to exploring and experiencing life without considering the consequences of my actions. When you've activated the greatness inside of you, a greater consideration is given to the elements connected to your decisions as well as the outcome.

A solution for the church is sustaining a connection with God. Supposedly, we go to church to serve God, but we are more concerned with serving ourselves. When this happens, God gets lost in the rubble. When church is designed to be about God, how do you lose God in the rubble? God is meant to be the focus, but often He is not—people are. People continually do everything that is against the principles and will of God. Why has that become acceptable? What if God judged our behaviors as they occurred, and we didn't have the next Sunday as an opportunity to do better or repent? There were immediate consequences to the actions that Adam and Eve took. Furthermore, they knew what they did was wrong, which was the reason they hid from God.

Sometimes, people have a degree of guilt from decisions that contradict what they were supposed to do. I don't know if my father harvested any guilt for his actions. He never told me otherwise. His behaviors were an indication that he was not connected to God, nor did he have an interest in being connected to God, as he did not change. He focused on pleasing his flesh, entertaining and pleasing others, and doing what he wanted to do. He made a career of it. When you are connected to God, you are not concerned with pleasing others, as greatness resides inside of you and you don't have any desire to ignore or remove it.

Man is not perfect. We cannot produce what God can produce. We are constant students of life, and this taught me to follow and trust God above man. Over a period of decades, through observation, I have learned to draw people to God rather than man. I don't need the focus to be on me, I want it to be on the spiritual relationship with God.

Dad had to work overtime with his entertainment—he worked hard to get and keep the attention of his audience.

People were drawn to the talents that my father had, and he was gifted. The problem was that my father was not displaying authentic actions when he ministered or living with the greatness that he was given. His inability to do so was one of the reasons a man with that much of a gift could not move beyond locality. God will never elevate you to the world. People have the ability to neglect their connection with God and gravitate to their naughty nature when there is entertainment and they see it as such.

There is a part of us that likes to be entertained. People are captivated by entertainment. That's why we go to the movies, sporting events, and so forth. We don't see every movie or attend every sporting event because some don't pique our interest. Before entertaining anything and everything, we need to ask ourselves what we like or don't like about these things. As you identify those things, take the time to understand the reasons behind your choices. Examine your motives.

There is a difference between being well known and being impactful. When you are not impactful in a positive manner, you don't need exposure. You are going to cause more harm than good by sharing negative or incorrect information. The best thing that could have happened to Dad is that his exposure was limited to a certain group of people. If you think about Adam and Eve, they were the only two people in the garden. God didn't fill the garden with people. And, while damaging, the serpent was limited to his exposure.

Adam and Eve entertained the serpent for a brief period of time. It seemed as though it was a moment of minimum dialogue, though irrevocable harm came from it. Generally speaking, when people make unfavorable decisions, it will completely expose the cunning and crafty characteristics and attributes they have, which mirror the serpent. When you have someone trying to talk to you about your core beliefs that contradicts what you innately know, before accepting it as fact, have that self-talk and ask yourself qualifying questions to determine its truth or value. Ask yourself what their intent is. And ask yourself if it is aligned with the Word of God. Greatness has a residence inside of you, so look within, as that is where you will find the truth.

You have to be able to identify those attributes and characteristics of individuals who don't deserve any exposure in your life. Don't give everyone access. Strive to be in tune with God so you can hear Him above the noise and deception. Learn to be confident in your own beliefs, or you won't recognize contradictions, chaos, or manipulation. If you aren't confident in what you believe, doubt will infiltrate your mind because you aren't secure. If doubt can creep in, so can the opinions of others.

If Eve had trusted God and what she knew, perhaps she would have paused and rejected the temptation. She would have been aligned with God enough to recognize contradictory words and phrases. And you can do this when you know what God has directed you to do. When someone is contradicting the Word of God and you entertain it, that person is insinuating that you do not possess the intellect or trust in God to know the difference. You are not resolute in your faith, and something you did let them know this. What do you think that is? You're listening.

Our biggest wins in life are not necessarily about who we let in but rather who we left out. Looking Within: Why We Don't Say No But Should is about trusting in God, yourself, and the greatness that resides inside of you because you innately know better. Take accountability for what you know. Take pride in the greatness that has residence inside of you.

You will meet countless individuals from various walks of life, dissimilar cultures, and more. You must know that everyone in the crowd is not in your corner. People are in your crowd because you possess something they have or something they want. This is a reason the church has to be careful, because we can be drawn into building a crowd without creating a spiritual impact on the crowd.

Just because you go to a church doesn't mean it is not a polluted environment in need of EPA, but no one checks because of its label. It is a church. The name protects it from questions because it's supposed to be good. As you walk through its doors, ask yourself what its actual purpose is. What are you gaining? Churches have positive optics; however, it is important to assess the environment, messaging, and behaviors of those leading it. Given I've been a part of church for so long, I learned to see beyond the label and the entertainment. I hear the word and observe the messenger. I pay attention to the work being done in the community and how well it serves people. During my life, history has displayed negative and derogatory leadership that speaks of one thing and does another. I've been in churches where spirituality is not the priority, yet, through everything, I have had access to learn the most valuable lessons. Those lessons have caused me to be better and rise above conflict, sin, and forgive others—even myself. And perhaps I was meant to experience all that I have so that I, too, like Adam and Eve could make the decision to do things my way or trust God.

I have attended church services that are astounding representations of places to worship, learn, and grow. There is accountability, organization, and the focus is on the Word of God—and, more importantly, teaching how to live according to the Word of God. You are fed spiritually, and it helps to keep you connected to the greatness that resides inside of you.

We are doing something right when people think of church as a place to grow in their faith, where progress can be measured and accountability is expected. When the people around you don't correct or challenge negative behaviors or issues, they become susceptible to repeating the cycle or becoming dismissive of those behaviors. If someone doesn't fix something, sometimes they may not consider it to be broken. We must care enough to hold one another accountable so that we can become better human beings. We owe that to ourselves. When everyone is doing the same thing or has their own skeletons, it can seem hypocritical or difficult to hold others accountable. If your church is the type of place to hold people accountable, that is a good place to start.

Here are a few things that can help you determine if church is helping you develop spiritually:

1. Is God the priority?

2. Is your purpose centered around God?

3. Consider the impact that God has had on your life. What are the fruits?

4. Have you seen spiritual growth and positive growth by attending church?

5. Are you compelled to practice what you are learning in church?

I have been impacted internally, and it drives me to serve in a capacity that represents what the church is designed to do—make a positive impact on humanity. If the Word of God is what we are teaching others and want them to live by, then the word of God has to govern the environment of the church. It is about honoring what is residing inside of you.

Society has gotten into the practice of isolating people who don't buy into or fit in the larger consensus. We can get caught up on the external movement without reevaluating the internal impact. If you believe that God can work inside of you, make the changes within you and then impact others. I have learned that it is not advantageous for everyone to look, work, and act a certain way, as it becomes about presentation rather than impact. Allow people to come as they are, wherever they are in their journey, and meet them halfway.

I would never have been able to preach the way I do today had I not returned home to Mississippi for my life lessons. I discovered that everything I hated or that hurt me was an intentional part of my life, and that is the way it was meant to happen⸺ so that I would learn. And you will learn, too, if you are open to it. It didn't happen immediately, as my maturity and growth took time, but if you are persistent in this endeavor, it will happen. As for the greatness that resided in me, I had to begin the journey to find it, understand its origin, and then activate it. Everything and everyone has a purpose. The manner in which we interpret the value may not have come from a situation or experience of our choosing, but it is undoubtedly there. It's the way we learn. It is the way we stop judging, blaming, hating, and destroying ourselves in the process.

The purpose Dad, Mom, Grannie, Bishop, Frentrous, and everyone in my life has had on me has been revealed. Contrary to what it may have appeared to do at the time, it ultimately made me become a better man of God, son, husband, father, and teacher. I'd given too much time and focus to the negative attributes of others that I thought were hurting me when their choices should have challenged me to be better in every area of my life, including in the eyes of

God. They were a gift. Adam and Eve were presented with the opportunity to become better as well; their strength to say no was put to the test.

During our journey, our experiences will require a great deal of thought and honest reflection to continually make sure we are working toward our destiny and not against it. It requires patience and persistence. To ensure greatness has residence inside of you:

1. Do a self-examination every step of the way.

2. Explore who you are and commit to who you desire to be.

3. Be satisfied with yourself.

4. Accept that everything starts with you, hold yourself accountable, and learn from experiences.

5. Have self-talk before and after making decisions.

6. Acknowledge your limits and work within God's structure.

7. Become secure in your relationship with God.

8. Understand greatness has residence inside of you.

When you are trying to alter your life for the better, the adversary or serpent will attempt to slither its way into your life and create chaos. Protect what you know is true.

When I made the exit from St. Louis and went to

Mississippi to pastor, I was going into an area where my father's reputation was widespread. I made the decision that I wanted to be a better person. Dad appeared to be a phenomenal preacher, and I will never diminish his ability, as it was his gift. What we do with our gifts is the question. What we do with the ability and authority to influence others is another.

I was angry with my father because I was disappointed with what he did with his gifts. He used them, but not the way he could have. I wanted Dad to use his gifts to positively impact lives, including for Mom, Frentrous, and me. I was fighting him and my destiny, so much so that I couldn't see how much he had that I could learn from that was good.

Ultimately, I followed the footsteps of my father into ministry but not into the totality of his life. I think over the years I only wanted him to be the things he wanted others to be. I wanted him to be the father I thought I needed because I knew his impact could have been substantially greater than what it was. We are human and will undoubtedly make decisions that are less than favorable or not always what others would want. We were forgiven for our sins—which means God knew we would make them. This was something I had to reconcile with my father as I forgave him. When my focus was given to the greatness inside of me, my focus was to be a better human being. It's not something you can stop striving for because life will continually challenge you to be better. As long as you have challenges, adversity, and serpents, you will be tested. Whether you can rise above it is up to you. I knew a very good preacher, but my father didn't let me get to know the good person that was there. We choose who we want to become and those we allow to shape us.

The most important aspect is to have moments of reflection in regard to the things you have experienced or people you've encountered that have influenced you without your permission. If you want to be a better person, you cannot ignore what you have experienced. When something or someone is diametrically opposed to what the Christian faith is about, protect what you instinctively know, the greatness residing inside of you, and your destiny.

Had I focused on business, financial gain, or notoriety in Mississippi, it may have been okay because I would have been seen as Johnson junior. People may not have said anything directly to me about what they thought, but they would have accepted me as an entertainer and looked past everything else. It was an easy path, but I wanted to influence the lives of humanity by example and not by verbalization. In order for me to accomplish that, I needed to look within. Don't look to become a replica of what is around you. Hold yourself accountable and others won't have to.

We all have the opportunity to be better. We have the choice not to be, too, because our life and free will is just that— it's ours. My Granddaddy Norman was a philanthropist. He was a musician and a giver. Where he lived in the South, Granddaddy made sure families had food, gifts, and things they needed, especially during Thanksgiving and Christmas. Granddaddy Norman was an incredible musician, but it was his kindness and compassion that made his reputation.

———————⟋⟍———————

I was nearly eight years old when Mom took us to her best friend's wedding in Rosedale, Mississippi at the Terrene Masonic Hall #3. I remember the blue building, right on the edge of the street, with four white pillars and a grass yard behind it. Dad was a Mason, and Mom was an Eastern Star, which is the sisterhood or female version that empowers members to impact the community. Mom was the maid of honor for her friend Minnie. Dad wasn't invited to the wedding because her friend knew what Dad was like, so he told Mom not to go, but she did anyway. When Dad entered the hall, his nasty facial expression let me know he was in one of his moods. He headed toward Mom in a heated, aggressive demeanor. She was sitting in a brown metal folding chair in conversation with some of her girlfriends. Frentrous and I were sitting to the left of Mom, who looked beautiful in her light blue dress. Enraged, Dad snatched Mom up by her neck and drew his hand back to punch her. Attempting to shield Mom, my brother and I jumped in front of her in time to take some of that punch. But it didn't matter, Dad wasn't done. He continued punching and slapping Mom, turning the reception into a big scuffle. Frentrous and I were fighting to separate them because Mom wasn't fighting back and it took some of the men and women to get Dad out of there.

That night, the drive to stay with family out in the country was reticent. I sat quietly with my hands folded across my chest. When I glanced down at my clothing, my little makeshift suit was stained with blood.

Word of what happened had already traveled to Dad's parents. The next day, Granddaddy and Grandma Johnson came out to the country and had a serious conversation with Mom.

It appeared they were trying to be discrete with what they had to say. They were sitting at Grannie's brown wooden table. I could see hands moving and that Mom was locked in and listening. I tried to listen in, since Frentrous and I were in the middle of it, but I couldn't hear everything. I suspected they were trying to help Mom strategize her move, but she didn't leave Dad at that time, so they left us. I wondered if Mom was given an ultimatum because I don't recall having any more interactions with them following that last plea.

One day, I asked Mom what Dad's parents said to her that last day I saw them. She revealed that Granddaddy Norman cautioned, "You take those kids and you run for your life and you guys don't look back this way."

Years later, Granddaddy passed in his sleep. Just a few months later, my grandmother passed by an aneurysm. They never reconciled with Dad prior to their passing. It seemed that he had done so much damage that he was disowned. One of the reasons I didn't want to disconnect from my father entirely was that their disconnection from him punished us, too.

Greatness must not be suppressed or obstructed. Hold

yourself accountable for who you are and whether you are aligned spiritually by doing the following:

1. Mentally commit to doing what is aligned with your spiritual principles and beliefs. I am human, so everything isn't aligned, but I work toward it consistently. Either you are going to have a high level of commitment or you won't. It takes work.

2. Making the right decision doesn't mean it will benefit you.

3. Be honest in assessing whether your decisions have had a positive or negative impact.

4. Accountability doesn't mean there are endless rules and regulations; however, it does mean you are not hurting anyone, including yourself.

When you hold yourself accountable, you are silencing the serpent, because it is not a part of the equation. Self-accountability removes the voice of the serpent, and the biggest influence that remains is you. Had Adam and Eve held themselves accountable, they would not have left room for the serpent to engage in the fabric of their lives and disrupt the greatness that resided inside of them. I had to silence the serpent. If I didn't, the serpent was going to have an influence over my life.

9.

GO WIN

"Not boasting of things without our measure, that is, of other men's labours; but having hope, when your faith is increased, that we shall be enlarged by you according to our rule abundantly."

2 Corinthians 10:15 (KJV)

~

God declared His creation of humanity as good. This statement alone provides humanity with a foundation to build upon. The task challenges humanity to go through life walking in the goodness that God has declared. This requires humanity to consistently rehearse what God has already established. Goodness has residence on the inside of humanity! What humanity does with it is a choice that God allows. The choice that humanity makes will determine the connection or disconnection from God. Adam and Eve made a decision that caused a disconnection, which led to the question of what if? What if Adam and Eve had cast down the words of the serpent? What if they had repeated what the serpent said to God before reacting? These what ifs can be clearly answered by looking at the Garden before the serpent influenced humanity,

Adam and Eve would have lived a life of peace, prosperity, and production had they remained in alignment with God's plans. They would have been winning because they would have accomplished what Paul said in 2 Corinthians 10:5: "Casting down imaginations, and every high thing that exalteth itself against the knowledge of God, and bringing into captivity every thought to the obedience of Christ" (KJV). Winning requires staying committed to God the creator of all things. When this commitment takes place, you eliminate the voice of the serpent that can show up in your peaceful and productive place. You consistently remember who you are in God, and you rehearse what God has declared concerning you. You stay on a path that keeps you connected to God and you invest in your inner man through study of the word, prayer, and serving. Each of these spiritual principles will lead you on the journey of making the choice to become what God has declared. When you are working daily on becoming more like Christ and walking in obedience to His voice, you are destined to win in every facet of life. God has given you every tool you need; utilize them on your journey to victory!

Had I not returned my focus to God, I was going to be at a place with both lowered expectations and morality. The scary part is that would have been accepted, given my environment. It seems we are always transitioning from one experience to the next. As part of that process, we need to take the time to distinguish and evaluate our standards to ensure we haven't lowered them along the way. The expectations of others should not impact the expectations you have of yourself. If your desire is to change and live a life aligned with God, determine whether you are going to stay married to an unhealthy identity or create a healthy new one. The big picture will reveal the results, so study it.

Consider what the people around you want. Is it more of the negative or positive? I asked myself, knowing who my father was, why invitations were extended for him to speak and sing at so many places. Was he trying to change humanity when the serpent made its entrance in his life? Or had that happened prior to becoming a pastor? As long as the serpent has your ear, you will not win. Did Adam and Eve win?

When it comes to spirituality, entertainment must not be the focus—your relationship with God is what is important, not how good you feel going to or leaving church. How you are living as a result of what you are being taught matters. If being entertained is the focus, it insults people who work hard to uphold the principles and precepts of God in which we preach.

Self-talk will cause you to entertain the reality of your motives. It makes you think! Ask yourself if your preacher helps impact or enhance your relationship with God. If not, say no to going through the motions and find one who does. No one can keep you from your relationship with God other than you. Are you practicing what you are learning or are you simply showing up and listening for entertainment and socializing?

When negative behaviors ensue for an extended period of time, it becomes an acceptable practice. "For the time will come when they will not endure sound doctrine; but after their own lusts shall they heap to themselves teachers, having itching ears" (2 Timothy 4:3 KJV).

Is what you are being taught having so little impact on your soul that it is not good enough without entertainment? God will draw men unto him, but we are drawing them unto ourselves and that is the problem. When spirituality becomes suffocated, humanity will be led astray. We are so willing to be led that we will accept being misled. I am not that eager to allow someone to mislead me, which is why I like to learn. People will use the Christian venue to build their notoriety. It has become a social environment in which kindred spirits attract one another, and church is not filled with perfect people. At the end of the day, it is my responsibility to stay true to the principles and precepts of God. The Word of God will stand forever. It is my responsibility to help you go win at life.

Once I had some time to decide as to what I was going to be and do regardless of influences to dissuade me, I was committed. When you commit to something, honor your word. The reason I remained resolute in following my destiny is that the choice comes from within. My life—my choice.

I had witnessed enough to know I would face some of the issues that pastors face, but I decided I would not make adjustments to my inner man. I was not going to attempt to fit in or make people comfortable with inadequacies. When you commit to being a better person and leading people to a better place, what logical reason do you have to deviate from doing the right thing? Why wouldn't you strive to be even better and step away from what you know is wrong? Eve made changes based on the communication with the serpent—no consideration to what God, her creator, told her. I am certain that the best way to impact others is to be a good person yourself. Do what is right. You can't make someone into something better or take them to a place you have not been. How can I lead people to make good decisions or look within if I haven't done it? If I hadn't experienced what I am suggesting or asking, what I preach would be a false narrative. My father preached a false narrative, and he had to live with that. He didn't make the choice to look within and change because other people made him comfortable.

I want people to communicate why they have selected our church. What is the purpose? What do they want to achieve? If I don't ask, I won't know how to help them overcome whatever they are facing. I can't help anyone connect to God on a higher level if I don't know where they are spiritually. Without knowing, it would be impossible for me to be as effective as I can be. I want people to reach the place where they release all of the negative issues holding them back from being great. I truly care about people. I don't mind someone leaving my church because they have different spiritual goals. People respond to people who make them feel comfortable— as well as uncomfortable. When you are in a place where you need to be comfortable, you are choosing to be complacent and your growth will end. You can't win if you aren't willing to face your reality and do the work.

<hr>

When you can impact others and convince people to stay connected to God, you are winning, because God is the source that humanity must have. He is the creator of all things. He knows all things. Most importantly, His desire for us to succeed supersedes any desires of any other thing created. Understanding the sacrifice that Christ made on behalf of humanity speaks to His care and concern for His creation. As it relates to the mistakes and failures we are going to have in life, God has given us the ability to overcome them and to be forgiven. This means that you have a choice in every matter. You don't have to give up. Reflect on what Christ has done for humanity and understand that, as individuals, we are striving to be what God has called us to be. We are his children, and we are human.

When I have days of discouragement, I remember and reflect on John 3:16 (KJV): "For God so loved the world, that he gave His only begotten Son, that whosoever believeth in him should not perish, but have everlasting life." It is His love, care, and concern that I cling to so that I can stay on the journey of winning. Winning in life is not a one-time event; it is ongoing. Too many people can't win because they see winning as an end and not as a constant process that we undertake in life. Disconnections matter. The serpent's conversation with Eve caused them to disconnect from God. They were already winning, and then they willingly deviated from their path. Adam and Eve were created with every resource and tool that they needed, just as we were, but their sins changed the path for all of humanity. Despite that, it is the material things as well as power and impact that we are consumed with even after God has given us everything. Like Adam and Eve, we want more. God said to them, name everything. He gave Adam and Eve power and dominion over all of His creations, including themselves, which is the reason they were able to fall.

Listen to people, collect information, and determine what you need to reject. The serpent wasn't talking to someone who wasn't intelligent, yet the serpent was crafty. The adversary was designed to get Adam and Eve off course. And that is its desire—to get us off of our course, the one God created. He ordered the steps of Adam and Eve and gave them explicit instructions. The only thing the adversary can do is work through you in order to get to you as it did Adam and Eve. When you know how to separate what God has said and what your flesh wants to do, you are winning. Winning derives from the inside out. Make decisions with passion and purpose in alignment with the Word of God. If you are winning because of what God has given you, you don't have to chase more because it will find you. The win was designed to draw it to us; we are positioned for it.

Since we were given the gift of autonomy to make decisions, it is our responsibility to eliminate or avoid conversations with serpents and negative influences. Stay connected to people and relationships that are good influences. Align yourself with those who are on the same page with the same purpose so you can positively encourage one another. Adam needed a support system, and when you have that, you are destined to reach the place God wanted you to be. Even after the bad decision Adam and Eve made, they created complexities. But they still had the same tools. God didn't remove them. The first thing that happened was their flesh became heightened, and they covered the flesh. Learning from them, it is our battle to suppress the flesh. That flesh will get us in trouble. It causes us to do things we should not because we are descendants of Adam and Eve.

When you overlook negative behaviors, it is not about Christianity. If you are not in a position to hold me accountable, and I am not in a position to hold you accountable, no one grows spiritually or matures, and we are appealing to our flesh. When someone's spirit is unsettling but that is who you are around, you have invited it into your environment. You can attract something based on who you have become when spirituality isn't a priority. Spirituality requires discipline and accountability. When you see something that is wrong, address it. If you don't, it diminishes the need for change. People should be drawn to church to ignite change.

During the following six years while I lived in Mississippi, I didn't think I was doing a good job because Dad never made any positive changes for himself, but directly and indirectly, he made me better. I was walking in forgiveness, and I was at peace. I had a clear illustration of what not to do and how not to treat people. He didn't change, but my presence caused him to become more discrete. Studying my father and learning how incredible a pastor he could have been made me want to complete the journey properly. I thought about my love for my family, passion for football, as well as my love for ministering and teaching. I couldn't help but want to win. Winning is staying the course, putting in the work, and knowing when to give whatever it takes so you can go the distance and reach your destiny. More importantly, winning is knowing God.

Being with Dad helped me understand the man that I didn't know, and finally the curiosity I carried for years had ended. My eyes were opened. For the most part, within the first two shows we performed together, I understood what he was all about. I had the opportunity to observe my father and the path he chose that contributed to his being lost. The quartet was everything to Dad. Had he been a good person and surrounded himself with good people, it probably would have taken him to heights unknown, but there was a prerequisite.

I enjoyed the travel, singing, meeting and ministering to new people, as well as learning more about myself and my journey in the process. I was free to grow in ministry, music, and as a man because Rochelle Johnson had a trump card that Joyce Johnson never had. If Rochelle told me not to go on tour or if there was a conflict that related to the priorities of my home, I would not have gone. That same respect had not been extended to Mom. Neither Rochelle nor Mom had any reason to use that card given that I'd maintained open and honest communication and held myself accountable. And yes, my father shared his platform with me, and it did impact my career. Not only did it provide incredible exposure and the opportunity to learn how to write songs, I was learning right from wrong. Good from bad. What to do and what not to do by looking within first.

The wives normally weren't in attendance when the quartet group traveled, which was a part of the problem. Knowing this, I had aspirations of elevating the group's level of spirituality. I wanted us to reach a broader audience through song. In addition to touching the lives of others, I wanted the words we sang to become a part of our daily lives. I wanted them to further impact us. That's what I believed people should see—we should have been that example. However, when I brought up the spiritual aspect, it was countered with laughter and jokes about spirituality. My father's laughter and jokes were the loudest, as it was intended to discourage deeper conversations. It became noise, a distraction from discussing the truth and who we were supposed to be. His goal was to keep us from looking at ourselves. The smoking, drinking, and profanity was nothing close to what one would have imagined. They had an impressive platform, but the following that came with it, or groupies, made it more of a fan club than a church congregation. I didn't know if I could be successful in that type of environment, but if I were ever to be a man of influence, especially to those in need, I couldn't walk away. I had to say no to all of that.

Dad had the tools and the gift to impact humanity. He had it, just as all of us do in some capacity or another. It was just that the meaning behind every song, from such a gifted writer, wasn't there. Working with my father taught me how to compose songs, but I sought ways to write songs through prayer. The spiritual inference, meaning, depth, intent, and impact was in every single song. I know this because they impacted me.

Initially, I pondered how the words and meanings came to Dad, because it wasn't imitating his life. He sang, "Though the mountain seems hard and sometimes in life's valley it gets dark, it's me, it's me O' Lord standing on your word again." I had to wonder where those words came from. Just because someone doesn't do right, doesn't mean they don't know right from wrong. I know Dad knew. He sang about it. But he wouldn't win in life if he continued living without faith.

Eve was wrong. The reason she didn't look within is because her free will had suffocated her obedience to God. Just as Eve agreed to try that forbidden fruit, she could have said no after reflecting on her instructions from God. I dug deep and thought about the ramifications of being that close to my father, but I was secure in my relationship with God; able to say no to anything that wasn't right. I was focused and connected to what God put in me. In doing so, the outcome would be successful.

One of the beautiful aspects of my life is that I finally came to know my father. The act of trying to reconcile my anger brought us together, and I forgave him. Dad was able to meet my son Kaleb and our daughter Kennedy, who was born in 2007. In the moment, and in the end, I can say that it was a privilege to tour and sing with my father. The irony of our relationships and experiences is that there are valuable lessons to learn or poor choices to make with each one. Mom and Grannie prepared me for the lessons I would need to learn from my father. They raised me to be strong, to know and trust God, and to forgive. Even though I tried to run from God, I knew where I belonged. I knew better, and I didn't have any excuses not to do better with my life. People often point out that their father, mother, or whoever never taught them anything, whether they were present in their life or not. I thought the same until I trusted God. Through watching the errors of my father's ways, I learned to be resolute in my faith when the serpent was staring me down. He also taught me to be resilient in the face of adversity, focused on God rather than man, and confident in my ability to overcome adversity and the power that forgiveness can have. Bishop's ineptness taught me that if you don't truly trust God when things become difficult, discouragement and doubts can emerge, causing you to deviate from one good path onto the wrong path. In following the path of my destiny, I learned how to win.

In August of 2008, I was at our church daycare talking with Mom when I received a call from my father's wife. She said, "Your dad is unresponsive. Can you get to Clarksdale?"

"I'm on my way." I got in my truck and drove to Clarksdale with my phone ringing non-stop and buzzing with people asking, "Is it true? Did your dad pass?" By the time I arrived at my father's house, I discovered that I was walking in with the county coroner. My father had a heart attack.

Dad was 54 years young when we buried him in three different counties. If I hadn't come back to repair our relationship, I would have been left with too many unknowns. The opportunity to say goodbye didn't exist. I didn't know why I had such a heavy pull to return home, but time has a way of revealing those answers. We had approximately 900 people at his musical night, nearly 1,400 people attended the viewing. When we returned to his church, there were chairs outside of the sanctuary and the rest was standing room only. People came from all over the state to pay their respects to my father. I finally realized that I had learned from one of the best. If you want to know how to prevent poor decisions or avoid taking the wrong path, you can learn a great deal when you study someone who does because you will have seen some of the consequences.

Although I was grateful that Dad and I took the opportunity

to reconcile our relationship to the best we could, I was disheartened that he never made an exodus from the path he chose. I don't know if Dad had a defining moment in his life that caused him to make the choice to lead and live the way he did, but he was a reason why I had to look within. When you have defining moments, you are meant to pause and evaluate why they transpired. What are you supposed to be doing now? Defining moments show up when it's time for you to make a turn. Pay attention to them.

After a handful of shows, I felt it was time for me to leave the quartet. Joining the quartet was my attempt to mend the relationship with my father and understand who he was. I had accomplished my goal. The last few shows and festivals exposed what Dad wasn't doing for the guys in the quartet. If we did a 45-minute set, we made practically nine thousand dollars, but Dad only paid us a few hundred dollars each. What he didn't know was that we played because we had passion and purpose. We wanted to minister through our music. They were a talented group of guys who had the chance to make changes and do things right moving forward.

Long before his untimely end, Mom won by forgiving Dad because she didn't live with anger or hate. She was the example that caused me to forgive Dad. When I did, I won, too, because forgiving Dad removed his ability to hold me mentally or emotionally hostage. I spent too many years being angry and hurt by his treatment of Mom and his lack of being there for me. I wanted to be a positive example for Dad and let him see the impact both he, Mom, and God had on me. I went from hating him to loving him. It wasn't my place to judge my father because, as Adam, Eve, and each of us, he would answer to God.

There is so much anger and hate in this world and we are not here to partake in it. We are here to contribute to what is good. We have the constant opportunity to be a healthier example—a better person.

After nine years in Mississippi, I had accomplished everything I had gone there to do. I was evolving into who I needed to be, which was the man God created me to be. I was taking care of my family, walking in my divine assignment, and I was winning. This is why it is important to search out and make sure you are on the right path and, trust me, you know. Often, we give information to others and ignore it ourselves. If it is good enough for me to tell you, it's good enough for me to practice it, too. And I am still climbing, in pursuit of being the best man I can be. That's a journey that doesn't end. We can always get a little better or do better.

Winning isn't about what you have; it is about who you are on the inside and whether you are walking in that divine place and purpose that God has for your life. Ministry had to be a priority. If your ulterior motivations take priority over ministry or doing what is right, don't do it. People need authenticity, especially on the path to know and trust God. They need the truth and individuals with integrity teaching them the Word of God. If the optics are more important, that is the wrong reason. People who are trying to better their lives place their trust in God. Furthermore, they live their lives according to the Word of God and don't need a false sense of direction.

As in any other industry, betrayal, hurt, and loss come with being in ministry. People think it's clean and easy, but it is not. If you study the Word of God, you will understand that ministry is messy. If you get into ministry, you can face personal discouragement, feel angry, or become disgusted; but it doesn't benefit anyone, including yourself. My father portrayed the messiest picture I'd ever seen. That is what I had to learn to overcome. If you sit around long enough, listening and accepting the negativity behind the scenes, you are entertaining the serpent and you will learn how to be that way. This is applicable to any aspect of your life.

Ten years after my return to Mississippi, and after prayer and consideration of my family, it was time to leave. I felt I had done what I was supposed to do at home. I had reconciled with my father before his passing and it changed me. Returning home was my time of maturity and training in ministry while pastoring my church. I became equipped and more knowledgeable about the Word of God as I developed into the man God wanted me to be. I was able to forgive my father so that I could experience that healing and know its power when I would ask others to offer forgiveness.

Entering ministry with the unfavorable experiences I had allowed me to search for peace and understanding through God. Otherwise, I would not have it. It helped me understand my choices in the military and why I was trying to defy my calling. God had long prepared me for my journey. For a period of time, I had every reason to abandon my faith; I hadn't seen God in a positive light. I didn't know God the way He wanted me to know Him because I was looking in the wrong direction. I had no reason to be angry with my brother because his intent was never to divide us. I should have applied the story of Adam and Eve to our relationship. Unfortunately, early on, the negative overshadowed anything that I could have deemed good. And, as with me, if you keep those negative sentiments over the good ones, you will only grow in anger. God kept the light on my path while Joyce Johnson and Rochelle Johnson never stopped inspiring and supporting me in my journey. I am no longer surprised by anything, nor am I afraid, as God has given me wisdom and strength to overcome and focus on what is right—what is His will.

I was winning when I realized how much my family supported me. When the people who know you the most can listen to you on Wednesday for Bible class and then again on Sunday for service, it speaks volumes. When people who know you best can sit at your table, eat what you are feeding them spiritually, and be proud to say they go to your church, you are winning. You are winning when you have positive spiritual influences, good people in your corner, and, more importantly, a relationship with God. When those who claim to love you show you they not only love you but they trust and respect you, too, that's winning! If people aren't receptive to who you are and they can't see the good in you, what is the benefit? Ask yourself what you are trying to accomplish. Have that self-talk so you can figure out how to change, because you can. If people are supportive of you and they know your behavior is not good, ask yourself why that is so. Have self-talk about that, too.

Being able to look down from the pulpit and see my cousins, Hattie Bell, and the family was a big deal. They were helping to thrust me forward at a time when it didn't seem anyone wanted to hear this young pastor, the little rock-thrower who returned home from St. Louis. They could see what God had done in and for me. At a time when I was not adequately prepared, my family refused to let the lack of support from others cause me to quit. My family was enough, and God was all.

It saddened me that Dad couldn't say that. His parents didn't go to his churches. Grannie didn't go to any of his churches, either. She went to her own church where she felt an authentic connection to the Word of God. Watching Grannie come through the doors of my church was something special. She was a Lekevie Johnson supporter. Her love and pride in what I was doing mattered more than one could possibly understand. But it stayed with me. It's still with me, and one of the reasons I aspire to be the best version of myself. You should aspire to do the same, be the best version of yourself, because it's there, waiting for you to claim it.

I didn't get this version from Dad, but it was embedded in me from those who were able to inspire me to be Pastor Lekevie Johnson, despite the challenges that I faced and the paths I tried to take early in life.

Today, I am the father of Kaleb and Kennedy, two incredibly loving children, who are proud of me. They are a huge part of my support system, as every time I look at them, they hold me accountable, though they may not realize it.

Being secure in my relationship with God allowed me to observe and learn a great deal without being negatively influenced to go against God. Dad taught me what my children need most from a father. His deficiency was instrumental in driving me to be a better father. And, yes, time teaches and heals if we are receptive and come to understand the power that forgiveness has for others—and for you. It's both cleansing and therapeutic. It was Lloyde Johnson who taught me how to be the best husband I could possibly become. My mother deserved so much better, and I wanted her to see that, after all of the pain Dad caused as well as the time, work, and investment she freely poured into us, none of it was wasted. I wanted her to know that she'd raised us right because she never let us depart from God regardless of how hard I tried. I wanted her to know that I love my brother Frentrous, as that is the way it should be. Out of the darkness was born the greatest desire not to listen to or entertain the serpent—not to ignore God.

It was my father who made me want to win at life more than anything else. His flaws taught me to be the husband that Rochelle deserves. He taught me to be the son that my mother deserves, one that will not cause her to feel devastation, only pride.

God has given us the gift of free will, and that free will

allows us to make the decision to be our best and trust God above man. When we know what we want out of life, it's up to us to use what God gave us and earn it. The only way we can win is by trying. We cannot win without looking within and knowing when we should say no. We cannot win without God.

We can sense when something is wrong and we can reconcile that feeling when we look within, the answers are there. It's better to do it than not at all. Looking within is a lifetime journey. It is something you must sustain and practice consistently, then you will see the difference in your life. Aspire to be your best and know when you should say no—say it firmly and with confidence.

What we entertain has to be in alignment with our journey or we will delay our victory!

Getting better daily requires mental rehearsal of what God has said concerning who you are.

Embrace the spiritual journey God has you on; ignore every voice that contradicts what you know God is doing in your life.

Often, we discover valuable information or insight in hindsight. If we take the time to look within ourselves to detect and correct these poor decisions, negative behaviors, emotions, and thoughts prior to the point that the damage has been done, we can alter our course for the better. Look within for those warnings that will protect you from others as well as yourself.

ABOUT THE AUTHOR

Lekevie Johnson is a native Mississippian and a former United States Marine who served a six-year term. The son of a preacher, he grew up in the church and had the privilege of serving in many capacities within the church. Some of his positions included percussionist, head of security and hospitality, as well as being appointed to Eldership. Lekevie Johnson preached his first message in 1998 titled, "Stay Focused." He was later licensed and ordained to preach in 1999. In July 2001, Pastor Johnson was called to Pastor Restoration Life Ministries in Cleveland, MS where he served as the shepherd there until February 2009. Pastor Johnson had the privilege of recording and singing with his father, the late Rev. Lloyde Johnson, in a Gospel Quartet Group from Mississippi.

Lekevie served as a member of the Mid-South Delta Leaders Tri-State Leadership Program at Delta State University in Cleveland, MS. Pastor Johnson received his B.S. in Religion at Liberty University, his M.A. in Christian Ministry Leadership, and is currently completing coursework for the Doctor of Education in the Christian Leadership Program at Liberty University Baptist Theological Seminary. Pastor Johnson was called to pastor Jericho Missionary Baptist Church in Urbana, IL in March 2009. In July 2010, he led the congregation in the purchase of a new worship facility. Under Pastor Johnson's leadership, the church has grown spiritually and numerically and 400 new members have been added to the church. Pastor Johnson led the church into a name change in March of 2019 to begin a spiritual fresh start. The new name of the church is Mt. Calvary M.B. Church, also known as "The Hill."

Pastor Johnson considers it a divine privilege to be a leader to God's people. He is compassionate about teaching the Word of God and watching God's people excel in their spiritual walk. He cherishes the opportunity and exposure to be a servant in the church. Pastor Johnson is the visionary and founder of the Lifeline summer camp and senior citizen program, both designed as a multicultural and diverse learning community that prepares adults and students for academic, social, and personal success in a safe and supportive environment.

Pastor Johnson currently serves as Moderator of the Fellowship Baptist District Association; he serves as the vice-chairman for the Champaign Fire and Police Board of Commissioners. Pastor Johnson is a certified instructor for the National Baptist Congress of Christian Education. He is the chairman of Social Justice for the Baptist General State Convention of Illinois. He is the former first African-American Varsity Head Football Coach for Centennial High School in Champaign, IL. Pastor Johnson is the proud husband of Lady Rochelle P. Johnson and the father of Lekevie Jr., Kaleb, and Kennedy Johnson, all of whom he adores.

Made in the USA
Monee, IL
06 December 2020